The (... to Deborah

Michael McGehee

Illustrated by Dorothy W. Newbert

A Liturgical Press Book

THE LITURGICAL PRESS
Collegeville, Minnesota

Cover: Design by Ann Blattner. Illustration by Dorothy W. Newbert.

1   2   3   4   5   6   7   8   9

Library of Congress Cataloging-in-Publication Data

McGehee, Michael David.
    The Gospel according to Deborah / Michael McGehee.
        p.   cm.
    Summary: Deborah gets the chance to practice her writing skills when her father, Luke, writes an account of Jesus' life and gives some of his chapters to Deborah to rewrite from a young person's point of view.
    ISBN 0-8146-2105-8
    1. Bible. N.T. Luke—History of Biblical events—Juvenile fiction. 2. Jesus Christ—Juvenile fiction. [1. Bible. N.T. Luke—History of Biblical events—Fiction. 2. Jesus Christ-
-Fiction. 3. Authorship—Fiction. 4. Fathers and daughters-
-Fiction. 5. Christian life—Fiction.] I. Title.
PZ7.M167525Go   1993
[Fic]—dc20   92-42659
                                                CIP
                                                AC

CONTENTS

CHAPTER 1

My name is Deborah. I'm writing this story to tell about my father and the book he wrote. His name is Luke. The full title of his book is "The Gospel According to Luke," but it's also called "Luke's Gospel" and sometimes even just "Luke." A gospel is a kind of book which tells about the life of Jesus.

I'm telling this story so that I can practice my writing. I think I would like to be a writer like my father. But writing is hard work. It's not simply a matter of sitting down with ink and paper and then writing whatever comes into your head. You also have to read books, think about what you're going to say, and read over your own sentences to make sure they say what you mean. Sometimes I can't get the words on the paper to agree with the ideas in my head.

It's not often that girls are taught to read and write where I come from. Here in Greece, and throughout the Roman Empire, boys are usually the only ones sent to school. The boys learn how to write and how to do arithmetic, but most people nowadays (that is, in the year 90 of our Lord) say that education would just be wasted on girls. Some people say that since girls will all become mothers and have families to look after, they don't need to be able to read and write. They just need to know how to cook and clean things up.

But I think that's a dumb idea. My father must have thought so too because he took the trouble to teach me the alphabet and how to read. And it was a lot of trouble for him and my mother. They had to teach me at home since the teachers don't usually have girls in their classes. I'm one of the few girls in our town who can write. In fact I can read and write better than most of the boys, including even those who are older than me.

My father has said that God gave all of us, men and women, boys and girls, different abilities. Some people are good at making things, or organizing, or teaching, or whatever. He said that we need to find out what things we're good at and then we need to do them. We need to use our talents the best way we can.

It was a couple of years ago that my father got the idea to write his book about the life of Jesus. After church one Sunday he was frustrated about something. He was talking to my mother while we were eating lunch. (My mother was still alive then. I will tell you later how she died.)

"Did you notice anything about the Scripture reading today?" he asked us.

In church we always have a reading from the Scriptures. We have singing, prayers, and a sermon too.

I said that I didn't notice anything about it. Mother said that the Scripture reading was telling about something Jesus did when he and his disciples were on a ship during a storm. She didn't notice anything unusual about it.

"But I noticed something strange," he said. "Remember last month when we heard the same story?"

We said we remembered. It had been the same story.

"Not exactly," he said. "The story last month was from a different book. And if you were paying close attention you might have noticed that the story was a little bit different this Sunday."

"Are you sure, father?" I said. "I remember both of the stories. A storm comes up when Jesus and the disciples are sailing across the Sea of Galilee. Jesus tells the wind to stop blowing and makes the sea calm again. Then he tells the disciples that they need to put their faith in him."

"Very good, Deborah," he said. "You have a good memory. But that's not exactly right. In the reading last month Jesus first calmed the storm, and *then* he told the disciples to have faith in him. But in the reading today Jesus told the disciples to have faith in him while the storm was still raging. Then, after he finished talking to them, he calmed the storm."

"You know, Luke," said my mother. "I think you're right. But I had never noticed that before. The stories are different."

Even though my memory is good, I couldn't remember back to last month in church. I didn't say anything.

"But I don't see that it really makes any difference," said my mother. "We all know that Jesus had the power to perform miracles. What difference does it make if Jesus calmed the storm before or after he spoke with the disciples about faith?"

"I'm not exactly sure," he said. "But I would like to know what really happened. I would like to know as much about Jesus as I could know. But when one gospel says something different from another gospel, I don't know which one to believe."

"I just don't see that it makes a difference," said my mother. "Jesus was the Son of God. He could perform miracles. I don't see that trying to figure out what really happened will help you understand Jesus any better. Jesus lives in our hearts now. We don't need to know about all those things that he did in the past."

My father just shook his head. He even stopped eating lunch. I could tell he was thinking about something. I was wondering if he had something else to say. But my mother interrupted him before he could speak.

"Don't bother getting interested in this, Luke. You've got enough to do at work and around the house to keep you busy. Here, have some more of these fried vegetables. I made them especially for you."

We didn't talk any more about the Jesus stories that Sunday. I thought that my father had forgotten about the differences in them. But I was wrong.

A few weeks later he brought up the subject again. We were eating dinner one night during the week.

"Did you notice anything about the gospel reading last Sunday?" he asked.

My mother and I said no. My father turned to me.

"Can you tell me what it was about, Deborah?"

My father often asks me questions. He says that answering questions is the best way to build up your memory.

"Just a minute," I said. "Let me think. Oh, yes, I remember now. There was something about John the Baptist and how Jesus was baptized."

"Excellent."

"But I don't see anything strange about that, Father."

"Not yet you don't, but let me explain. That story about Jesus being baptized is how Mark's Gospel begins."

"All right," said my mother. "But what's unusual about that?"

"It's unusual because there's nothing about Jesus being born, or about his family, or about what he did when he was a boy. We've all heard stories about Jesus before he was baptized, but Mark's Gospel doesn't tell us anything about them."

"You're right," said my mother. "But what difference does it make?"

"I still don't know if it makes a difference. But I can't help wondering why Mark didn't tell us about Jesus before he was grown up. It could be that Mark didn't think that those stories were important."

"Maybe he didn't know the stories about how Jesus was born or about what he did when he was a boy," I said.

"Good point, Deborah." He looked right at me. "But then doesn't that make you wonder why he didn't know those stories? Didn't he talk to people who knew Jesus before he was baptized?"

"I never thought about it, Father."

9

"And I still don't see that it makes any difference, Luke." My mother wasn't very interested in what he was saying. "Jesus is alive in the Church. He is alive in our hearts. We don't need to bother with those things that happened so long ago."

My mother talked about things happening a long time ago because it really has been a long time since Jesus lived on earth. It's been ninety years since Jesus was born. That means it's been about sixty years since he was crucified and resurrected. That does seem like a long time. To me, anyway.

It was two weeks after our talk at dinner that my mother got very sick. She wasn't the only person in the city who was sick. Dozens of people seemed to be sick, and even sick in the same way, during that month in the summer. Her skin felt hot, her head ached, and she was thirsty all the time.

No one in the city knew what to do for all the people who were sick. Some people, mostly grownups, got better, but many others got worse. Children and older people started to die of the sickness. Men and women from the church came by to pray for my mother. My father and I prayed too. But I guess that God decided it was time for her to go to heaven.

A few days before she died, a lot of red spots, about the size of small roses, swelled up on her skin. I'm glad that none of them came out on her face. Her face was still nice to look at. But after the spots came out, she stopped remembering me or my father. She would sleep and say things to herself. Then one day, when I was out buying our food for the next day, she died. My father was with her.

It was a terrible experience. Even knowing that other people in the city were going through the same thing didn't make it any easier. It seemed like everyone we knew had someone in their family die. Four families in the church had a child or baby die because of the disease.

I don't know why these terrible things happen.

For several months after Mother's death, my father didn't seem very interested in life. He still did his work and we still went to church, but he wasn't as happy as he had been when Mother was alive. He used to spend a lot of time sitting by himself. I guess he was thinking about something.

About the only thing that could get him interested in talking with other people (and me) was when he was thinking about the different stories in the Scriptures.

"You know, Deborah, time is running out," he said. It was early one morning while I was sweeping the floor and he was getting ready for work.

"Running out for what, Father?"

"Running out for learning the truth about what happened when Jesus was on earth," he answered. "The twelve apostles have all died. All of the people who knew Jesus when he was alive are either very old or dead now. If someone wanted to learn what Jesus really said and did, he would need to start doing his research very soon."

He stood by the door ready to leave our house. The sun was just starting to come up.

"When you say 'someone,' Father, do you really mean yourself?"

He smiled at me.

"I always thought you were a smart girl."

He left the house.

After that day I knew that he had made up his mind. He was going to write a book about Jesus. People who are used to having a lot of books or going to a library may not realize how much work this was going to mean. But my father knew that he would have to travel away from home. He would need to talk to all kinds of people and look in all sorts of books that churches had in their libraries. He knew that the work would take months, maybe even years, to finish.

During this time he also decided something that made me very happy about his plan. Even though my father could have sent me away to my uncle so that I'd be raised with my cousins, he decided that he and I were going to stay together. If he stayed at home, I would stay with him. And when he had to travel, we would travel together. Most girls never get the chance to travel, but I was going to be one of the lucky ones.

One of the first things my father did once he made up his mind was to tell it to the church. He told the church when it was his turn to preach the sermon. He gets the chance to preach because he is a "deacon" at the church.

A deacon is one of the leaders in a church. Deacons lead the prayers, do the teaching, and give the sermons. They also visit the sick. Both men and women can be deacons. In addition to those jobs, they also have charge over the money (what little our church has anyway) and decide how it will be spent on those who are needy. The deacons in our church say that money should be given to people who need it. They don't believe that money should be saved up or used to buy expensive things for the deacons.

I've heard stories that there are some churches where the leaders really do spend some of the church's money on themselves. My father even said that it was true.

"Deborah, one of the worst things about some Christians is that they get greedy. They use money, even other people's money that has been given to the Lord, to make themselves rich."

I said that was terrible.

"You're right. Jesus always talked about sharing and looking out for one another. But some leaders in the church take money and live as if they didn't care for anyone but themselves."

Well, back to my story. When my father's turn came to give the sermon, he told the church about his plan to write a book about Jesus. He explained that this was the right time to start.

"There are only a few people left alive who actually heard Jesus teach and knew him," he said. "And they won't be around that much longer. We need to get an orderly account of Jesus' life so that our children and grandchildren will know what he said and did."

Next he explained how he felt that the Holy Spirit was leading him to do this. Others in the church must have felt the same way too. In fact the other deacons came together afterwards and arranged to give us enough money to buy whatever paper and ink he needed for his writing.

I imagine that some people may not think that paper and ink were much of a gift. In fact I've heard that there are places where paper is cheap. But throughout the Roman Empire today paper is very expensive.

Our paper comes from Egypt. To make paper Egyptian workers first go into the swamps and gather a special kind of plant called papyrus. Then the stalks of the papyrus plants are cut into thin strips and glued together in sheets. These sheets are squeezed between heavy blocks of wood until they're flat, and then rubbed until they're smooth. It takes a long time to make paper.

Books are also very expensive. The paper is expensive because it is so hard to make. (In fact, because paper costs so much, when children learn to write, they usually do their first lessons and homework with pen and ink on broken pieces of clay bowls and plates. There's always plenty of that stuff.) But books are expensive not only because paper costs a lot, but also because the whole book has to be written by hand. There isn't any quick way to make a book. It can take a scribe several months of full-time work to finish a long book.

Our church only owns a few books. We have about ten Jewish books, which have been translated from the Hebrew language into the language we speak, Greek. We also have a few other books which only Christians use. The Christian books were all written in Greek.

It might seem strange to you that we use Jewish books in our Christian church. I know that when I first heard that Jews and Christians shared some of the same holy books, I thought there was something wrong. This happened a few years ago.

"They shouldn't be using our holy books," I said to my father. "Let them use their own."

"You've got it backwards, Deborah. Many of the books that we use as Scriptures were written by and for the Jews. But because Jesus was a Jew, and because we believe that he is the Savior of the world who was promised in books like Genesis, Isaiah, and the Psalms, we look upon those Jewish books as Christian books. Those books are full of prophecies about Jesus Christ."

"But then why don't the Jews give up those books since they tell about Jesus? It seems to me that the Jews either ought to become Christians like us or else give up their books which make prophecies about him."

"You're saying that because you haven't read the books we're talking about. Christians who read the Jewish Scriptures say that some passages are prophecies about Jesus. But Jews who read the same passages say that they don't see anything about Jesus at all. Because the writing in them is so hard to understand, Christians and Jews can read the same holy books and get two different messages."

"But why doesn't God show them that they are wrong?"

My father was quiet for a moment.

"Hmmm," he said and paused. "And why doesn't God show us everytime when we're wrong about something?" He paused again. "I don't think that it's our place to tell God how to run other peoples' lives. God works with all of us, Christians and Jews and people who believe in other

14

religions. The Apostle Paul said that God is at work leading all people to himself. I think it's our job to show love to our neighbors no matter what they believe. When we do that, we can leave the rest up to God."

From that time on my father has made a point of explaining the Jewish religion to me. He has said that you can't understand who Jesus was unless you understand who the Jewish people are. Because of that, in the rest of the book, I will try to say something about the Jewishness of Jesus and the people who knew him.

In addition to the Jewish books like Genesis, Exodus, the Psalms, and the Prophets, our church also has some books that only Christians use. We have copies of some letters by the Apostle Paul, some pieces of paper which have stories about Jesus, and, most important of all, a complete copy of the Gospel According to Mark. Our copy of Mark is less than ten years old. My father said that when he became a Christian, no one had even thought of writing a gospel. As far as we know, Mark was the first person to write a gospel.

Given my father's hope to write a gospel which would be more complete than Mark's, my father planned that we would first travel to Palestine and see if we could find anyone who had known Jesus when he was alive. ("Palestine" is the Roman name for the area where Jesus lived; it's usually called Israel in the Jewish books.) After we had talked to all the people we could find who still remembered Jesus, we would come back home. Then Father would write his gospel and explain what Jesus had really done and taught.

It was a good plan. The only problem was that it didn't work out.

We were about ready to start packing, and had already talked to some captains of ships about how much it would cost to sail from Greece to Palestine, when two missionaries visited our church. Even though deacons are the leaders

15

of local churches, there are some church leaders who travel all over the world preaching the good news that God loves us. These are the missionaries.

Both men and women can be missionaries. Many times they are husband-and-wife teams. When they come to a city, they find out where the Christians are. If there is a church, the Christians arrange for them to stay in homes and make sure that they're looked after. (If there's no church, the missionaries try to start one.) The missionaries usually preach at churches and visit with as many people as they can.

The missionaries who came, Priscilla and James, were married. They had just come from the church in Antioch. Antioch is in Syria, the country just north of Palestine, and is one of the largest and most active Churches in the world. My father had planned for us to sail to a port near Antioch and then walk the rest of the way to the city. It's only about fifteen miles.

Priscilla and James were both very old. Their faces were browned and full of wrinkles. You could tell they were old. Her hair was a snowy white. It was hard to tell about James' hair, since so much of it had fallen out, but what was left was mostly gray. The skin where his hair used to be was smooth and shiny. The rest of his skin was wrinkled like his wife's. I wondered if they had been alive long enough to have known Jesus. But my father said they weren't quite that old.

On the same day my father heard about them and heard that they came from Antioch, he arranged for us to get together with them for dinner on the next evening. One of the ways that we show we're Christians is by giving hospitality to strangers. But Father was also hoping to get information about where we should go in Palestine to meet people who remembered Jesus. While we ate, he explained about his plan to write a gospel.

"I'm sorry," said the old missionary James when my

father finished talking. "But I'm afraid it's already too late to do the kind of research you're thinking about. I don't think there's anyone left who knew Jesus."

"James is right," said Priscilla. "I don't know anybody who could help you. It was just last year that the only person in the Antioch church who remembered Jesus died. She was a very old woman."

"But there must be others left," I said. My father didn't speak. "Since it's only been about sixty years ago that Jesus went up to heaven, there must be some people left who knew him. Our church has a lot of people older than sixty."

"But you're talking about two different groups of people, Deborah," said my father. "There probably are lots of people left in Palestine and Syria who are older than sixty. But that doesn't help us any. We want to talk with people who can remember being with Jesus. We need to meet men and women who can remember what he was really like. Those people who never saw him or who were too young to remember anything about him couldn't help us."

"And don't forget the war," said James. "During the Great Jewish War—it was about twenty years ago, Deborah—the Romans killed thousands and thousands of people in Palestine. Some of the worst fighting was in the very areas where Jesus had preached."

"Many of the people who might have remembered Jesus were killed in the fighting or died in the famines after the war," said my father.

"Too true," said Priscilla.

"You said that the last person in Antioch who remembered Jesus was dead," said my father. "But wouldn't there be others left farther south?"

"I don't think so, Luke," said Priscilla. "You see, we had traveled through Palestine a few years ago. We walked through many of the places where Jesus had been. We never met anyone in a church who could remember Jesus."

"It was a depressing journey," said James. "Probably the saddest sight was Jerusalem. I can remember Jerusalem when it had almost half-a-million people. Back when I was a boy the markets were full of food, the streets were full of children, and the Temple stood on the mountain top above everything. But everything's gone now. The Temple has been destroyed. There's only a portion of the outer wall left. The beautiful homes and buildings have been torn down. And only a few people are left. They live in small houses built from the ruins of happier days."

After this depressing dinner, Priscilla and James left. My father sat by himself looking out the window. I was giving up my hopes of being able to travel. It wouldn't make sense to spend the money to travel to Palestine when there wasn't anyone left for us to talk to.

I was right.

"You know, Deborah," said my father the next day. "I think we'll have to change our plans. My idea was that we would talk to eyewitnesses of Jesus' life. I wanted to ask questions about what he said and what he did. From the people who had actually been with him, I wanted to find out what he was like. But I guess it's too late for that now."

"Are you giving up your idea of writing a gospel, Father?"

"No. But I've had to re-think how I'm going to write it."

"How will you do it?"

"Well, at the church we've got Mark's Gospel and some shorter writings that tell about Jesus too. Other churches probably also have writings about him. My plan will be to read over everything I can find about Jesus, pray that the Holy Spirit will guide me, and then write down what I think is the most orderly and accurate account of Jesus' life."

"When shall you start?"

"We'll start today."

That afternoon we went over to the church and started

reading the materials in the church library. The first thing to do was to find out exactly what was in the library. Since we already had Mark's Gospel, Father decided he would use it to give the basic outline of Jesus' life. Then any extra stories that we found that weren't in Mark's Gospel would be put into the right spots in my father's version.

I thought my father would start writing that night. But after a couple of weeks of reading and thinking, he hadn't written a single word. I wondered when he was going to begin. Then, during the third week, he started writing. But the first thing he wrote was an outline. He said he had to get organized.

Now the hardest part of being with someone who works quietly—and who wants you to stay quiet too—is that you get bored. My father was excited about what he was doing, but I didn't have much to do. I could read, but I wanted something more interesting to do while he was reading and writing.

After he had finished the outline for the first part of his book, I told him that I was getting tired just sitting around in the library. (I said "tired" even though I was really getting bored, but saying I was "tired" seemed more polite. He also doesn't like the word "bored.")

"But I like having you with me, Deborah," he said.

"And I like to be with you too. But I just don't know what to do with myself."

"I'll tell you what. I'll figure out something you can write on while I'm working. That way you'll be able to practice your writing."

"That sounds all right."

He drummed his fingers while he thought.

"I think I know just the thing," he said after a minute or so. "You've always been good at making up stories. While I work on the gospel, I'll tell you stories about Jesus that are going to go into my book. Then I'd like you to think about the stories and try to imagine how someone your own age, or about your age, might have acted if they had been there."

It sounded like a good idea to me.

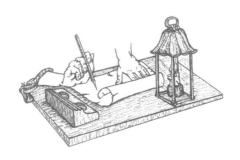

CHAPTER 2

T he next day my father had a specific suggestion for me.

"Deborah, why don't you try writing your first story based on this one from my gospel? It comes from one of the papyrus rolls in the church's library. Mark doesn't mention this story in his gospel, so you may not have heard it before. But it's a good story and lets us know a little about what Jesus was like before he grew up. It tells about something Jesus did when he was twelve. See if you can tell a story as if you were one of Jesus' friends."

I liked my father's idea. While he was deciding what else to put into his gospel and writing, I came up with my first story. I imagined what it would have been like if one of Jesus' friends had talked to me.

Saul's Story

(Luke 2:39-52)

Jesus, the son of Mary and Joseph, is a friend of mine. He and I are the same age. My name is Saul. My family lives in the village of Nazareth.

My father is a carpenter. Jesus' father is a carpenter too. Because our hometown is so small, I've known him since we were both little. But Jesus and I only became real friends several years ago when our fathers were working on a big building job. We've been friends ever since. He and I go to the same school and sometimes work together when we help our fathers.

It's hard for me to tell you about Jesus. I mean, what would you say about a friend of yours? How would you describe one of your friends so that other people could understand what he or she was really like?

I could start off by saying that he's well-behaved. But then you might get the idea that he's a tattletail, or a sissy, or a wimp. And he's not that way at all. Jesus is respectful to grownups and friendly with the other kids. He can get along with almost everybody. I don't know how he does it.

I could go on to tell you that Jesus is intelligent. But don't get the idea that he's a smart aleck though. Just because he's smart doesn't mean that he has to be stuck-up. He's good in reading at school, and he's also willing to help other boys learn things when they don't get it right the first time. Girls, of course, don't go to school.

Jesus and I are both learning to be carpenters. Our fathers are teaching us the trade. We are working as apprentices for them. They're both experts at doing things like putting wooden roofs on houses or making furniture. It is hard work being an apprentice carpenter. The carpenter who's your boss makes you carry the boards and fetch things for him. This can be tiring, especially when the boards are heavy.

But the hardest part of learning carpentry comes when you actually get to do something yourself. You can't help making mistakes. It can be very frustrating. Sometimes I try to saw the wood too fast or to hammer nails without making sure that the nail is standing straight under the hammer. Because of things like that, every now and then, I mess

up the wood I'm working on. That wastes time and money. On top of that, to help me learn, my father then makes me do the whole job over again if it's not done properly.

But I'm not the only one who has to do things over again. Jesus sometimes makes mistakes too. It's not that he gets in a hurry and makes mistakes because he's rushing, but his mind sometimes wanders on a job. He starts thinking about something, or humming or singing to himself, and then forgets what he's supposed to be doing. Now and then I've seen him jam his saw or smash one of his fingers with a hammer.

Unless you've ever had a hammer smash one of your fingers or thumb, you may not be able to imagine how much it can hurt. My father and the other carpenters yell out certain words whenever this sort of thing happens. Since my father does it, I guess that it's all right at times when you're really upset. (What I can't understand is why my father doesn't like me to use those words when we're at home or when our neighbors are around.) Jesus, on the other hand, doesn't swear at all.

I can remember one day when I thought he was going to, though. He was nailing two boards together and humming some song to himself. I could see that he was paying more attention to the music than to the hammer. Then, in mid-hum, his hammer missed the nail he had aimed for. It came down right on his thumb. I waited for him to start swearing. But he didn't. His face went pale, he put the hammer down, and walked over to a chair. I could see his thumb swelling and turning red. He sat very still for a couple of minutes. He might have been thinking, or swearing to himself, or maybe he just felt sick.

When his face was back to its normal color, he stood up and went back to work. Later on, when we stopped to drink some water, he admitted that he should have been concentrating on his work. He didn't stop his humming after that, but I could tell that he was paying more attention to his work.

But we boys don't have to work all the time. Many afternoons, if there's no school or carpentry to do, we go outside the village and play. We like to have contests in running, jumping, or wrestling.

I'm one of the best runners in the village. With my long legs I manage to win almost every time I race. Jesus is not quite as good at running as I am, but he's better than me when it comes to wrestling. Because we're used to carrying boards and tools, we've got strong arms and shoulders. Neither one of us is any good at jumping.

I have to say one other thing about Jesus. He's a good sport. When he loses in a race or wrestling match, he doesn't accuse the winners of cheating. He also doesn't whine and make excuses about what happened. Seeing him act that way has made me less likely to get upset when a race doesn't go the way I had hoped. I've also never seen him try to start a fight because he's mad about losing. And since he's so good at wrestling, he doesn't have many kids who try to start trouble with him.

Even though Jesus and I are friends, there are times when he acts more like a grownup than a kid. One of these events was only a few months ago last spring. It was during Passover. The Passover is a holiday feast that we Jews celebrate as a reminder of how God works. During the Passover meal we think back to the time when our ancestors were slaves in Egypt. In their misery they had prayed to God for help. God then sent Moses who led the people out of Egypt into the Promised Land of Israel.

Everyone who has the time and money likes to go to Jerusalem to celebrate the Passover holidays. Since our family had been saving all year for this, we planned to make the trip. It isn't every year that we can afford to go. Since Jesus' family was also going, we decided to travel together with them. We would be part of the dozen or so other families from Nazareth who were traveling together.

It takes almost a week to go from Nazareth to Jerusalem. The distance is around sixty miles. Sixty miles may not seem very far to you. But when you're having to walk, and go up and down hills, you cover the distance rather slowly. There's also a lot of other people on the way. (Jews from all over the world want to go to Jerusalem for Passover.) You can't help getting jostled and slowed down by the crowds of travelers and merchants.

Our families walked next to one another. That is, except for Jesus and me. He and I had the freedom to walk on our own. We sometimes played with other boys or strolled over to the other groups of people who were also traveling to Jerusalem. We liked to hear the old men tell their stories about what life used to be like. But we usually just walked by ourselves and talked.

I've mentioned before that Jesus sometimes talks like a grownup. By that I mean he says things that I can't always understand. While we were walking, he said that he was anxious to get on with "his father's business." I couldn't understand what he was talking about. After all, he is learning how to be a carpenter. That has to be "his father's business." But what could he mean by wanting to get on with it? He's still too young to work by himself.

After five long days of walking we finally saw Jerusalem. The city is in the mountains. Jerusalem is huge. Since I had never seen it before, I wasn't prepared for the size. There were thousands and thousands and thousands of people there. I don't even know the words to use when numbers get that high. The arithmetic we learn is mostly for counting, adding, and subtracting the numbers you come across in daily life. Many people never count above one hundred during their entire lives. Still, whether you believe me or not, I heard someone say that Jerusalem had over two hundred of thousands of people. It would be easy to get lost there.

Once we arrived, our parents gave us lectures about not getting lost. They told us to stay with them. We were not to wander away in the crowds. Jesus and his family left us soon after we entered the city. They were going to stay with one of Mary's relatives. We would spend the week with my mother's parents.

When we ate the Passover meal, the Seder (which is a sort of thanksgiving dinner), our grandfather told us the story of the Jews in Egypt. On every Passover this story must be told. We must not forget. Grandfather went on to tell us that God was still looking after us all.

A few days after that we left to go back to Nazareth. My family, Jesus' parents, and the other folks from Nazareth met outside Jerusalem so that we could walk back together. The roads were crowded with other people returning to their hometowns. I had to spend the day walking with my sister. She had almost gotten lost one afternoon, and my parents told me that I had to look after her that first day.

That evening, after we had walked about ten miles, Jesus' mother Mary came over to see our family. The sun had gone down, but it was still light enough for people to be setting up camp and cooking. We usually just sleep in the open. I was walking up to my parents after getting some water from a stream that was near the road. I could hear what they were saying but no one had seen me yet.

"Beth," Mary said to my mother, "have you seen Jesus?"

"No, I haven't," said my mother. "But he might have been walking with Saul and his little sister. You know how they like to do things together. Jesus was probably with them."

"But he wasn't," I said when I came up to the group. "I didn't see him all day."

"I wonder where that boy is," said Mary. She left us.

A little later, when it was dark, Mary's husband Joseph came over to where we had a small fire. He spoke to me.

"Saul," he said to me, "did you see Jesus today?"

I said that I hadn't seen him since we got into Jerusalem almost a week ago. My sister and I had looked for him while we were walking but hadn't seen him and we figured he was with someone else. Joseph then went over and spoke privately to my father.

The next morning Mary and Joseph arranged for all of us from Nazareth to meet together for a few minutes. They wanted to know if anyone had seen Jesus the day before. None of us had. Mary and Joseph then explained that they would have to return to Jerusalem and look for him. They assumed that he must have become lost in the city.

Since I could remember Jesus talking about how he

wanted to visit certain places in Jerusalem, I asked Mary and Joseph if I could go back with them. (It also seemed like a chance for adventure.) They said it was all right, my parents said it was all right, and we left in a few minutes. Mary and Joseph didn't have anything to say to me on the way back.

We arrived in the city during the late afternoon. We first went to Mary's relatives. None of them had seen Jesus in the last two days. They assumed Jesus had returned with his parents. Since it was almost dark by this time, we didn't try searching for him. Mary's relatives put us up for the night.

The next day we started looking in the places where a boy would be most likely to get lost. We tried the markets, we went through shops, we walked around the city walls, and we passed near the barracks of the Roman soldiers. (Boys like to walk by the soldiers to look at their horses.) We asked a few people if they had seen Jesus. But since he looked like so many other boys in Jerusalem, no one was able to help us. It was a long, frustrating day.

Our next day of searching took us to some more unusual places. We walked through the poorer sections of Jerusalem. Then we went into the richer areas. Still no sign. We were tired and getting ready to quit for the day when I remembered something.

"Jesus once said that he wanted to study in the Temple," I explained. "He wanted to hear what the famous teachers told their classes when they gave lessons about the Law."

Even though we were tired from all our walking, we dragged ourselves to the Temple. You have to walk up the mountain to get to the Temple. And once you're at the top, you have to find your way around the grounds. Certain parts of the Temple grounds are only open to men, so we had to leave Mary outside while we looked in the Men's Courtyard. Mary looked in the Women's Courtyard since

children are usually there. We didn't see him in the court-yards.

As we left through the main gates to the Temple, we looked down the outer sides of the buildings. In the shade made by the walls and columns we noticed several groups of men sitting together. They were classes meeting for their lessons. We walked past four of the groups before we finally saw Jesus.

He was sitting with a group of well-dressed men. The group he was in looked less like a class of students than a meeting of teachers. They were talking about something. I could tell the men were very important by the clothes they were wearing. They were dressed better than the other groups. (I've often been told that important people always wear expensive clothes.) I thought they must have been priests or lawyers.

Joseph, Mary, and I came near enough to hear the conversation, but we didn't say anything. It was just like being in school except that grownups were the students. In our schools one person (usually, but not always the teacher) asks a question. Then the others in the class try to answer the question or else explain why the question isn't phrased properly. The smartest kids sometimes say that the question being asked isn't "the real question" or say that there's some better question to ask.

Here at the side of the Temple we saw that Jesus sometimes asked and sometimes answered questions. Several of the teachers must have liked him because they said things like "Good point" or "He's got you there." But most of the teachers only smiled.

Finally Mary walked over to Jesus. All the men turned to look at her. (It isn't normal for women to interrupt men when they're talking.)

"Son," she said, "why have you caused your father and me so much worry? We've been looking for you three days now."

I could tell that she was upset.

Then Jesus said just the sort of thing you wouldn't have expected. I thought he would make up an excuse or apologize. That's what I would have done.

"Why did you need to look for me?" he asked. "Didn't you know that I would be in my Father's house?"

Most of us there didn't have the slightest idea what Jesus meant, but some of the teachers thought this was a fine answer. A few laughed. Several of them nodded at Jesus when he left with his parents and me. I guess they didn't realize he was only a carpenter's son. Some of them must have thought he was somebody important.

I wondered whether Joseph or Mary would spank Jesus for going off on his own. But nothing happened that night or on the trip back. Joseph had a private talk with Jesus, but all I heard was Joseph saying that it wasn't right for Jesus to make his mother worry.

The walk back to Nazareth was long and tiring. It was starting to get hot during the days. The roads were still crowded with travelers.

Jesus has been somewhat changed since we came back from our visit to Jerusalem. He seems more thoughtful and quiet. But he still continues to learn carpentry. And we boys still play together. But I can't help wondering whether Jesus intends to go back to Jerusalem someday.

"That's a good story, Deborah," said my father after I read it to him.

I think he was surprised about how it had turned out.

"Is there some way I should change it, Father? You know, to make it better?"

"Well, you might have told a little bit more about the Temple and Jerusalem and the Passover. I'm sure most people outside Palestine don't know what went on in the Temple."

"But that's the kind of thing they could ask a grownup about. And besides I don't know that much about Jerusalem and the Passover either. But what about the other things in the story? Did I make Jesus seem like a real boy? That's the main thing I was trying to do."

"I think you did. But there's nothing about him hitting his thumb with a hammer in any stories I've ever read."

"I know that. But, since he was a real boy, he had to learn things just like anyone else. That's why I put it in the story. It's not because I think it really happened, but it's there because I want people to know that he was a person just like any of the rest of us."

"That's interesting, Deborah." He paused. "In fact that may be the only way to write about Jesus. Because we can't go back in time to see Jesus, maybe all our stories about him only tell us something about what one person thought he was like. It could be that no story ever really tells exactly what happened."

He was thinking again. I interrupted his thoughts.

"But what advice do you have for me? How can I make my stories better?"

"Practice, Deborah. That's the way to learn how to write. Your stories will get better."

CHAPTER 3

Within a few days my father had written another part of his gospel and done more work on his outline. Father had thought that the story about Jesus calling his disciples in Mark's Gospel was too short. There were too many unanswered questions about why Peter and the others became disciples. Things just seem to happen so quick in Mark's Gospel. When my father found that one of our scrolls at the church had a longer account of Jesus meeting Peter, he decided to use that story. I imagined what it would have been like if the Apostle Peter had a daughter named Sarah.

Sarah's Story

(Luke 4:38-39 and 5:1-11)

My father is a retired fisherman. He didn't retire because he was getting old but because he has changed jobs. He will sometimes joke and say that he used to be in the fish business but that now he is in the people business. His name used to be Simon, but now everyone calls him Peter. Jesus the Prophet gave him that new name.

My name is Sarah. My mother—her name is Sarah too—and all my brothers and sisters and I live just outside the city of Capernaum. Our city is on the north shore of the Sea of Galilee. I like living next to Capernaum. There are always so many things to do and see in the city. The city has soldiers and sailors, priests and prophets, merchants and travelers. It is full of people. When I go into Capernaum with my mother to help her with the shopping, I spend most of the time holding her hand and staring at all the interesting people. She says that she has to drag me through the market place. She says that I get so nosey that I forget to keep walking.

Our house is near the beach. We can go to the beach anytime we don't have work to do. I like to go swimming. My father used to take us to the beach. While we would swim, he would do work on his fishing boat or untie the tangles in the nets. The thick threads that make up the nets regularly get twisted together and that means that someone has to straighten out the tangles. But if it was a really hot day, he would put off the work until sundown and join us in the water. He likes to swim too.

But he doesn't go with us to the beach like he used to. In fact he doesn't even live with us anymore. That makes it hard for us sometimes. He has gone off with Jesus and some other people from Capernaum to be a preacher.

This doesn't mean that we don't see him any more. Whenever he has a couple of days to spare, he will come to visit us. On these trips home he brings my mother some money and sometimes even small presents for us kids. Of course the presents aren't very expensive. And our mother still complains that we would have more money if he had stayed a fisherman. But we manage to get by. We hardly ever get new clothes or sweets, but we appreciate things more

now than we used to. We also get along better than we did before my father met Jesus. Still, I do miss the sweets.

It was about six months ago that Jesus came and asked my father to join him and the other disciples in spreading the good news. When my father tried to explain it to the family, he said that he had never—but wait a minute, let me tell you the story from the beginning.

We first met Jesus because of my Grandmother Ruth. She's my mother's mother. Grandmother Ruth must be very old. Even she's not sure how old she really is. Her face is full of wrinkles, but she still laughs and likes to play with us children. It seems like the older she gets, the more she likes children. She lives in Chorazin, a city a few miles to the north of Capernaum, with my Uncle Jethro and his family. Grandmother Ruth had come down to Capernaum to visit us. While she was here, she got sick.

Her face became pale and her skin felt hot. We put her into bed. During the hot afternoons (it was in the summer), one of us children stood by the side of her bed and fanned her. Mother tried to cool her by putting wet pieces of cloth on her forehead. Sometimes Grandmother would talk, but it was always in such a weak voice that I could not understand her, even when I could hear that she was saying words.

There was nothing we could do for her. After a few days her fever made her so sick that she wasn't able to recognize any of us. Even when her eyes were open, it seemed like she couldn't see. Sometimes she would call out the name of my dead grandfather. That made me scared. Was she seeing his ghost? After that my father walked up to Chorazin one morning to tell Uncle Jethro and his family about how sick she was. He must have thought she was going to die. A few of them came down to help us look after my grandmother.

While all this was happening, the Prophet Jesus came to Capernaum. He was planning to teach in the synagogue. Many of the people in our town had already heard stories about Jesus. Wherever he went strange things were supposed to have happened. He was also known because of the stories he told. Some folks even said that Jesus could make sick people get well.

But people are always saying that kind of thing about prophets and religious teachers. They are supposed to be such great and powerful men. But whenever they finally get to town here, whenever you actually can see them, they turn out not to do or say anything all that special. After a few of these holy men had come through Capernaum, my father told us not to believe everything we heard.

"These modern prophets and miracle men are really just fakes," he told us once. "They're not like the old prophets. We won't have any more prophets like Jeremiah or Amos."

He was right about all the modern prophets we met before Jesus. But he was certainly wrong about Jesus.

One afternoon, when Jesus had finished teaching in the synagogue, he walked past our house. I had seen him once before in the market place when he had bought some fruit. I think he had bought some oranges. There wasn't anything unusual about the way Jesus looked. He wasn't tall like a giant. He wasn't handsome like a king. He didn't have long, white hair like some of the other holy men. He looked like an ordinary person who was about the same age as—or maybe a little younger than—my father. I saw Jesus when I was looking out the window. I called to my mother and told her that Jesus the Prophet was walking by the front of the house. My mother had been crying because Grandmother Ruth was so sick. When she saw Jesus, she called out to him.

"Please, sir," she said from the open front door. "Do something for my mother."

Then several of my brothers and sisters and cousins ran over to Jesus to ask him to help Grandmother Ruth. My father watched the children run over to Jesus but he didn't say anything to Jesus.

Most of the holy men who pass through our town won't do anything for the poor people. They stay in the fancy houses with the best families and eat only the best food. They spend their time with the rich. When poor people ask for help, these phonies say that they're too busy or pretend that they don't hear what people are saying. But Jesus didn't act like any of the false prophets.

He did not walk past the house. Instead he turned and entered the front door. Since our house was crowded with relatives waiting for Grandmother Ruth to die, he had to squeeze his way up to her room.

When Jesus stood next to her bed, he reached down and touched her cheek with his hand. I could see the sweat shining on her wrinkled skin. He stood there for a minute or so just looking at her. Maybe he was thinking about how much her family loved her.

Then he spoke out loud. He told the fever to depart from

her. He told her that she was going to be healed. It was an odd thing to say.

Although we were glad to hear Jesus say all that, we thought it would be some time before she would actually get better. Lots of people know what it's like to wish that someone sick will get well. We didn't think that anything would happen because of Jesus' words. We were wrong. Just as I was starting to wonder how long it was going to be before she got better (and even if she was going to get better), Jesus began lightly patting her cheek. He was telling her to wake up.

She opened her eyes. He smiled at her.

"Thank you, sir," she said and started to get up.

My mother was surprised at all of this.

"Please, Mother," she said to my grandmother, "lie down again. You mustn't strain yourself."

"*Lie down again?*" laughed Grandmother Ruth. "Not until I have to."

She laughed again. I could tell that she wasn't acting normal. My mother was frightened.

"Don't you understand?" Grandmother asked. She looked at those of us in the room. "I'm healed. What can I do to show you?"

Then she had an idea. She made Jesus sit at the table and then went into the pantry. In a few minutes she came out with bread, cheese, and water. She offered these to Jesus. (It's one of our customs to offer guests something to eat when they stop by.)

Jesus ate a little bread and a little cheese. He drank some water. But he didn't say very much. My father, as the oldest man in the house, sat next to our guest Jesus. He ate a few bites of bread, but not much. He also didn't say much, except about the weather. It was still hot.

All of the children in the house came into the room and looked at Jesus. We also came over to Grandmother to give

her hugs. When Jesus and my father seemed to be finished, Grandmother stood by asking them if they wanted anything else.

Jesus left after he finished drinking the water. We didn't see him again until he came to ask my father to go away with him. When Jesus left, my mother and father made Grandmother go back to bed to rest. She didn't want to go.

As I said before, my father used to be a fisherman. He spent his time working outdoors. He was also the strongest man I ever saw. By himself he could pull up a heavy net full of fish that usually required the strength of two big men. He can still lift me with one hand.

But it wasn't always good that he was so strong. You see, he often loses his temper. I remember once when he was mending one of his fishing nets in the house. He said it was too hot to work outside. Fishermen usually work on their nets outside, near their boats. He was trying to get some tangles out but wasn't doing a very good job of it. That was making him mad. He also kept stabbing his finger with the metal pin he was using to untangle the knots. You could see little spots of blood on his fingers. That made him even madder. And when the pin snapped in two, his anger exploded.

Even though he wasn't praying, he started calling upon God to do something or other to the net. He was so angry that he began tearing the net in two. He ripped some parts of it. My mother rushed into the room where we children had been watching him work.

"*Simon!*" she said. "What do you think you're doing? Using the Lord's name in vain. And in front of the children!"

He glared at her with his angry, red face. I thought he was going to say something to her. But he didn't. He threw the net on the floor and left the house.

In about an hour he came back. Just by looking at his face, you could tell that he was sorry for what he had done. He called the whole family together. We children and my mother were on one side of the room. He was on the other side.

"I'm sorry for what I did today," he apologized. "It was wrong of me to lose my temper. It was wrong of me to say the things I said. You know that I love you very much. I'm sorry."

Once he cools down, my father has always been the kind of man who's willing to admit that he did something wrong. We came over to him then and hugged him and told him that we loved him. Mother did the same thing. She asked him what she was supposed to do with him.

After that my mother made some honey cakes for the family. They are her special treat for us children. When we ate them, my father told us stories about the big fish he had caught or almost caught. In his stories it's always the biggest ones that get away.

It was many days later that we saw Jesus again. The sun had been up for several hours, but it was still morning. I was afraid that my father was going to be angry again. You see, my father and his partners—James, John, and Uncle Andrew—had fished all night and hadn't caught anything. They were all tired. When they're tired and haven't had any luck in fishing, they often take out their frustrations on one another. We kids keep out of their way.

The four of them were sitting on the sand next to their boats. They were quietly pulling out the strands of seaweed that were entangled in the nets. None of them were speaking to one another. They looked disgusted with everything. We children sat several yards away and watched them work. We always do this.

Just then I noticed Jesus walking down the beach. There was a small crowd of people following him. Apparently he was going to teach a lesson outside the synagogue. I suppose the synagogue hadn't been big enough for all of them. When my father and brothers had gone to the synagogue to hear Jesus, they complained afterwards that the building was too small. It had been hot too. Most of the people following had come from Capernaum and Gennasaret, a nearby town.

While I watched my father yank the seaweed from his net, I wondered where Jesus was going to speak so that all the people could hear him. Jesus then walked over to my father's boat and asked to borrow the boat.

"You might as well borrow it," replied my father. "It doesn't seem to be very good for fishing. Not for me anyway."

Jesus then asked him to row it a few yards away from the shore. The people stood on the shore while Jesus sat in the boat. Jesus then taught one of his lessons. I don't remember everything he said but it was a lesson about how God cares about us. I've heard some preachers, who are called "holy men," talk about God in such a way that God sounds like Someone You Would Never Want To Meet. But Jesus talked about God in a different way. I liked listening to him.

When Jesus finished the lesson, the people went back to their homes. Jesus thanked my father for taking him out in the boat. Then he said something strange to him.

"Simon, if you take your boats out into the deeper water to the east and cast your nets there, you'll catch your fill of fish."

As soon as I heard that, I wondered what my father would do. You see, he thinks he's the world's best fisherman. And he positively hates to have anyone give him advice about how to fish. He often gets into arguments with his partners—and they're good fishermen—when they tell him what they think needs to be done to improve their luck. But now Jesus (a carpenter!) was giving my father advice about fishing. I wondered what he would do.

My father's face started to turn red, but he kept his temper. He probably remembered what Jesus had done for Grandmother Ruth.

"Look here, sir," he said. (I could tell he was restraining himself.) "We worked very hard last night and we didn't catch a thing. But if you *really* think we ought to go out and try again, we will."

He looked at Jesus. Jesus nodded his head. He wanted them to try again. When Jesus looked away, my father rolled his eyes. But he still said, "Let's go," to his brother Andrew. Then Uncle Andrew and my father got into the boat, shoved off, and sailed out to the deeper waters.

Since I know something about how my father thinks, I could tell that he was hoping that Jesus had given him bad advice. I mean, even though he wanted to catch fish, I also knew that he wanted to keep his idea that he's the world's best fisherman. He was willing to take the boat out to try to catch something, but he was hoping they wouldn't have any luck. I realized he was hoping to show up Jesus. He wanted Jesus to be embarrassed in front of the people on the beach.

When they were out far enough, he and Uncle Andrew threw the net into the water. After a minute or two, which everyone knows isn't really long enough for a good cast, they started pulling the net back up. My father knew it hadn't been in the water long enough. In fact, I saw him give Andrew a wink. He was trying to embarrass Jesus. I felt a little ashamed of him. After all, Jesus was only trying to help.

Then I noticed the muscles start to bulge on Andrew and my father. They were having a hard time pulling up the net. I suddenly realized why. The net was full of fish! They couldn't haul it into the boat by themselves. They shouted to the shore for James and John to come help them in the other boat. After the four of them worked for a few minutes, they finished pulling the net in. Both boats were now full of fish. I was even afraid they might sink. They didn't sink, but the boats moved very slowly towards the shore.

As soon as the boats landed, my father jumped from his and splashed through the water while he ran to Jesus.

He flopped down in front of Jesus. You could see his hands shaking.

"Please, sir," he said. "Go away from here. I'm too much of a sinner to have you around."

Jesus stood still for a moment. He looked at my kneeling father. He looked at my father's three partners. They were standing next to the boats. They looked like tired, sweaty fishermen who had been up all night. (And that's just what they were.) Jesus smiled at something he was thinking.

"Don't be afraid," Jesus said. "From now on you're going to be fishers of men. I want the four of you to follow me."

Father stood up. He didn't look at anyone on the beach. He stared at the sand. But there was something different about him. Then he motioned for us children to follow him as he starting walking home. We followed.

At home he made us all come together in one room. He explained that he was going to have to leave us for awhile. He was going to travel with Jesus as a "disciple." (A disciple is someone who is sort of an assistant and sort of a student to someone else who's a leader.)

"Do you really have to go away, Daddy?" I asked.

"I'm afraid so, Sarah. But it won't be forever. And I'll come back to visit you whenever I get the chance."

My mother was quiet for about a minute. Then she spoke.

"Simon, I realize that you think this is the right thing for you to do, and I don't want to discourage you," she said. "But how are we going to get along without you?"

"I know it will be hard, but the Lord will provide for our needs. We will all be looked after."

My mother didn't know what to say. She was still and didn't look at him or us. The room was quiet.

"Just what do you know about this Jesus?" she finally asked. "Do you think that you can trust him?"

"Of course, I trust him. You remember what he did for Grandmother Ruth? And the kids told you about catching the fish today?"

She nodded.

"I'd like for all of you to understand why I'm doing this," he went on. "But I don't really understand it myself. Right now it looks like I'm leaving my work, my home, and our whole way of life. But it won't be forever. This is not something that's going to be easy for any of us. But I feel like this is the best way I can serve God."

I didn't really understand what he was saying, but I knew that I didn't like the idea of my father going away. I was about ready to cry. I could see that my mother felt the same way. There were tears in her eyes.

"Simon, Simon," she said. "Whatever am I going to do with you? I pray that the Lord will be with you. And us."

Father then hugged each of us children. He whispered something into my mother's ear. He kissed her and walked away. He was gone.

After I got over the shock of him leaving, I was afraid. I was old enough to understand why my mother was worried. At first I wondered whether we would ever see him again. Would we have enough money to get by on?

But I don't worry anymore. You see, Father and the other disciples often come back here to Capernaum. We see him more often than I had at first thought we would. He tells stories about things Jesus has said and done. He also brings us food and money. But I wish we could all live together again.

During the first few weeks after my father had left, I was mad at Jesus. I believed that he had stolen my father. I sometimes wished that we had never met him. Too many things had changed since he came into our lives. But I don't feel that way anymore. In fact, now that Jesus is becoming famous throughout the country, I realize what an honor it was for Father to have been called by Jesus. Sometimes I even wish that Jesus would call me to do something for him.

A few months had passed from that day when all the fish had been caught. One day my father came home unexpectedly. He usually sends a message before he comes home. But on this particular day he just walked in the door.

He said he wanted to tell us that he had a new name.

"What did you say, Simon?" asked my mother. She had just come out of the kitchen and was wiping her hands.

"Don't call me 'Simon' anymore," he laughed. "My new name is 'Peter.' It means 'the rock.' Jesus gave me the new name. It means that I'm as strong as a rock."

"Peter, Peter," she said. "Whatever am I going to do with you?"

"You can come over and show me how glad you are to see me."

With that he gave us children a wink.

"Deborah, this is really good," said my father Luke. "Where do you get your ideas?"

I told him that I didn't know.

"But there is one thing that I have a question about," he said. "Where did you get the idea to describe the Apostle Peter this way?"

"I just followed your example, Father. I read over what the church has that talks about Peter. Mark's Gospel tells that Peter swore and lost his temper. I figured that if he acted that way after he met Jesus, he must have been like that before he met Jesus."

"All right."

"And I also wanted him to seem like a real person. But I don't mean to show any disrespect. I remember hearing that the Apostle Peter was killed because he followed Jesus."

"That's true, but it was a long time later. If there had ever been a real daughter Sarah, she would have been a grown woman, maybe even a grandmother, when Peter died. She would have had a long time to get to know her father."

"There was another thing I wanted to do. I wanted to show how hard it must have been for Peter to leave his family to follow Jesus. Mark's Gospel and your gospel just say that Peter left everything behind."

"That's true. But writers always hope that readers think about what they're reading. No one can ever tell the whole story. As soon as readers try to read between the lines, though, they'll realize how hard it must have been for any of the disciples to follow Jesus. None of them had an easy choice."

CHAPTER 4

A few days later my father Luke was trying to write out one of the speeches which Jesus had given in his travels.

"It's hard to find out what Jesus really said, Deborah," he told me that night after dinner. "I have Mark's Gospel and some other records, but they don't always agree with one another."

"But you knew that even before you starting writing, Father. You planned to set the record straight."

"And that's just what I will do, but it means that I have to use my own judgment in deciding what Jesus really said or did. That is, I'll have to use my own judgment more than I thought I would need to. It's like in your story about Peter and his daughter Sarah. You chose to describe Peter as a man who had a quick temper. Well, of course, Jesus didn't have a quick temper. I'm sure of that. But when I read passages from Mark or other material, I have to make decisions about what I'm going to write about Jesus in my gospel."

"You mean that even you aren't always sure about what happened?" He nodded. "You don't always know?"

"It's not just that I *don't* know. It may be better to say that I *can't* know."

"We can only do the best we can, Father."

"That's certainly true," he said and laughed. "I do have something you might want to use as the basis of another story, Deborah. It's a sermon that Jesus gave when he was in a field near the mountains. It doesn't show up in Mark, and I heard someone say once that Jesus gave a sermon like it on a mountain. He probably gave the same talk many times as he traveled. See what you can do with it."

Joel's Story

(Luke 6:20-26)

I am Joel. I live with my grandfather in a cave in the mountains of Judea. My mother died when I was born. My father died a few years ago.

My grandfather does not live in a town or on a farm. He is a prophet and lives with several other holy men on the side of a mountain a few miles from Jerusalem. They usually sleep in the good-sized cave they call home, but they also have tents for when the weather is especially fine and they want to feel the fresh air.

A few weeks before he died, my father took me to my grandfather's home. My father explained that he knew he didn't have much time left to live. There was some disease in his lungs. He used to cough all during the night and for most of the day. He felt like he couldn't catch his breath. When he finished telling all this to my grandfather, he asked, "Will you look after Joel?"

Grandfather replied that he would. He also said he would look after my father until he died. The next month was terrible. I was too young to understand everything that was happening. All I knew was that my father was getting sicker and sicker. As soon as he would lie down, he would start coughing. When we first arrived at the tent where Grandfather was living, my father had strong coughs. But within a week he could only gasp and sputter. About this time he wasn't able to stand up anymore.

One night I went to bed and heard my grandfather trying to talk to my father. Father looked as if he had something to say, but he was never able to say it. He kept coughing too much. Next morning I woke up later than usual. Grandfather hadn't called me when the sun came up.

I could tell that there was something different that morning, but it took me a few minutes to figure out what it was. It was quiet. My father wasn't coughing anymore. I thought for a minute that he had been healed. That's what I had been praying for.

I ran over to the place where he was sleeping. But he wasn't sleeping. His eyes were shut and he wasn't breathing. I knew he was dead. I reached over and touched the skin on his cheek. It was cold. I don't remember when I started crying, but I was crying when Grandfather came over and put his arm around my shoulders.

"Cry as much as you want, Joel," he said. "But you can also be thankful to God. Your father will never have to suffer again."

I guess you could call my grandfather a prophet. We spend much of our time talking to travelers who are going to Jerusalem. I also have charge of the goats which belong to the holy men. Sometimes we go into the smaller towns in the area so that Grandfather can speak to the people. We don't go into Jerusalem. Grandfather says that the people there are too far gone.

A lot of people have the mistaken idea that prophets always talk about the future. This just isn't so. A prophet's real job is to speak God's word to the people of his own time. (A prophetess does the same thing for the people of her own time.) Now there were some prophets long ago who could foretell the future, but my grandfather and the men who live with him are not that kind. They only talk about what's happening now.

A prophet is never a popular person. One of the main things that prophets talk about is how wicked people are. They warn the people that God is becoming angry and that there will be punishment for disobeying God. No one likes to hear that sort of thing. Many years ago Grandfather had gone into Jerusalem and preached that sort of thing near the Temple. He was arrested and beaten up and sent out of the city. He doesn't intend to go back.

Everyone can tell that Grandfather is a holy man. He has a long, white beard and long, flowing, white hair. Because he is out in the sun so much, his face is dark brown, in fact, almost black. But it is not his beard, or hair, or face that make people realize that he is a prophet. It is his eyes.

I really can't describe those eyes. Their color is such a dark brown that they sometimes look all black. Whenever he looks another person in the eyes, that person gets the feeling Grandfather knows everything that person ever did. No one can look into those eyes for very long. I certainly can't. I've never seen Grandfather lower his eyes when he started looking at someone.

Jobal, another holy man who lives nearby, once told how a lion tried to attack Grandfather. The lion was on a rock ledge above him when he saw it prepare to pounce. Grandfather looked it right in the eyes. The two of them stood there, looking at one another. Then the lion looked away and washed its front right paw. Then it rubbed its paw against the side of its face. In another minute or so the lion turned and walked away.

I once asked my grandfather if this were a true story.

"I won't say that it's true," he said. "And I won't say that it's false. All I'll say is that it isn't important."

That answer didn't tell me what I wanted to know. But that's the way Grandfather often talks. It could be that something like it had happened but that Jobal had exaggerated. Stories about holy men are often exaggerated to make a point about how powerful they are.

It's true that there are some people who call themselves "holy men" but who deliberately make up stories to show how great they are. Many of them are prophets because they can make a lot of money. Prophets like that usually live in the city. They have expensive tastes in clothes, food, and houses. They have lots of followers who like to hear what they say. Prophets like my grandfather and Jobal live in the country. They eat vegetables and cheese. They never have anything fancy to wear. Almost no one pays any attention to them. Grandfather says that's just the way things are.

I would like to be a prophet when I grow up. But Grandfather says that it isn't enough to want to be one. He says that God must want me to be a prophet. He says that God will have to call me.

"Does that mean I'll get to hear God's voice?" I asked once.

"That's not what I mean at all," he replied. "God calls men and women to be prophets in many different ways. You might hear God's voice. That's what happened to the boy Samuel when he became a prophet. You might see a vision like Amos. But most likely you will look back at all the things that ever happened to you, and then decide that God made them happen to you because you were supposed to be a prophet."

He looked at me with his almost black eyes. His eyes looked into mine. I turned away.

"Don't want to be a prophet, my child," he said. "Today a prophet must be separated from the common people. It's a lonely life. In fact, the reason we have you look after our goats is so that you'll be able to be a shepherd when you grow up. Being a shepherd would probably make you happier."

For some time now we had been hearing stories about a man from the town of Nazareth named Jesus. The travelers we saw often said that he was also a prophet. Some people even said that he could be the Messiah.

"What's the Messiah?" I asked my grandfather once.

"I really don't know, Joel," he answered. "Some of the priests say that he will be a prophet, priest, and king rolled up into one person. Many of the lawyers think that he is going to be a king like King David of old. Some of the teachers think there will be two Messiahs. But most of the people think he will be a general who will lead us Jews in a great war to get rid of the Romans who rule our country. Most people expect him to take charge in a war of independence from the Roman Empire."

"What do you think, Grandfather?"

"I don't even know what I think. All I know is that when the Messiah, or messiahs, come, the world is going to be changed so much that it will never be the same again."

One afternoon, when we were sitting by the edge of the cave to keep cool, our neighbor Jobal ran over to our cave.

"Come out. Come out," he called. "That fellow Jesus is going to speak down in the valley later today. We need to get going if we want to hear him. At last we'll be able to hear him."

We left the cave. Both Grandfather and Jobal were curious about what sort of man Jesus was. Was he a real prophet or a fake? Neither one thought that he might be the Messiah. We walked briskly down the hillside and into the crowd.

Jesus was sitting on a smooth rock surrounded by people from the nearby towns. Very near him were about a dozen men who seemed to be his friends. He was talking with them and was obviously waiting for the crowd to settle down. Because of Grandfather's appearance, the crowd moved aside as the three of us approached Jesus.

We sat down about ten feet in front of Jesus. While we had walked up, neither Jesus nor his friends had paid any attention to us. But when we were settled, Jesus turned and looked Grandfather straight in the eye. I could tell that they were sizing one another up. I wondered when Jesus was going to lower his gaze, but then two of the disciples came in between Jesus and Grandfather. One began talking to Jesus. The disciples, that is, the friends Jesus had with him, were motioning with their hands and trying to show the crowd that it was time to get quiet. Grandfather turned around to look at the people behind us. His glance can often make things settle down.

After the crowd became still, Jesus began his sermon. Maybe "sermon" isn't quite the right word. "Sermon" sounds so boring and impersonal. I'm not that old but I've already heard some pretty boring sermons in my life. But Jesus didn't talk that way at all. I felt as if he were speaking to me alone. He wasn't using big words that I couldn't understand. He wasn't like the priests who sometimes make it seem that they're better than everyone else. And he wasn't like one of the holy men who so often make people feel sad because they're not as good as they should be.

On the other hand, Jesus said some strange things. He started out by talking about how certain people were "blessed." To say that someone has been blessed is another way of saying that they are happy. Jesus said that poor people, those who were hungry, and those who wept were blessed. Then he said that he felt sorry for the rich, for people who laughed all the time, and for those who were famous.

I'm not sure what Jesus was getting at. He was saying just the opposite of what we normally say. Right now we say that we feel sorry for those who are hungry and talk about how the rich people have been blessed. I didn't understand his point. Was Jesus trying to get us to think that what happens in our daily lives doesn't matter? Or that it doesn't matter very much in comparison with God's will? Or was he saying that after we die there will be another world where God will reward people who suffered on earth? I'm not sure.

Still there were some things he said that I did understand. At one time he talked about how we should give to others so that God will give to us.

Now of course that doesn't mean that you can make any deals with God. That is, you give away something small and then expect that God will give you something big in return. God will reward us for generosity but it may not be in a material way. Giving things to others could mean giving time or showing kindness as well as giving something that costs money. And I suppose that the gifts God gives in return may be as simple as the good feeling that you get because you've done something right.

When Jesus finished talking, Grandfather walked up to him and spoke for a few minutes. I wish I could have heard, but in our culture children aren't supposed to listen in on conversations among adults unless they're asked. After they spoke together, Grandfather nodded and walked away. He did the same thing when he had met another famous prophet, John the Baptist.

As we walked home, neither Jobal nor Grandfather had anything to say. There were questions I wanted to ask, but

I could tell that the two of them were thinking about what Jesus had said. We had almost reached our home when Grandfather looked at me. He was ready to talk.

"Well, Grandfather," I said, "what do you think about him?"

"That's an interesting question," he said and smiled. "You could just as properly ask what he thinks of me. Certainly he is a holy man. But what do you think of him?"

"He speaks much better than the other prophets we've heard. Yet you can tell that he wasn't educated in the city. He seems to be more of a country person, but from someplace in the north. I liked listening to him. There was a lot I didn't understand, but I did see his point about how we need to show love to other people even when they're not lovable."

"And why is that, my child?"

"Because everyone is able to love people who are lovable. The hard thing is loving people you don't like or who don't like you. Only those who truly are the children of God can do it."

"You said there were some things you didn't understand. Tell us what were some of the other things you *did* understand."

"I liked it when he said that however you wanted other people to treat you, you needed to treat them. That only seems fair. If you expect others to be considerate towards you, you ought to be considerate towards them."

"Yes. Go on."

"But you know, Grandfather. I feel like I've heard something almost like that before."

"That is true, Joel. There are passages from our Scriptures where Moses gets the credit for saying something similar. You can find the same sort of thing in the book of Leviticus."

"Then Jesus is just repeating Moses?"

"Not exactly. Obviously Jesus has read the words of the great Jewish prophets from the past, but he has picked out the passages which he thinks are most important for the people today. That is what all teachers have to do. The message Jesus has comes from our own Jewish heritage."

We were home now. I was tired after all my walking and I didn't feel like doing my chores. I'm supposed to walk over to the spring and get the fresh water for the evening. I needed to check on the goats too. And another job I have is to gather wood for our fire. But I felt like sitting and talking.

"Why did Jesus say that a blind man couldn't guide a blind man?" I asked out loud and then, because no one spoke, I answered my question myself. "The answer is obvious, but Jesus gave it. They'll both fall down because neither one can see. Why did he bother to tell us all that? Everyone knows that."

Grandfather spoke now.

"Jesus was telling a parable. A parable tells a story with some hidden message that you're supposed to figure out. When Jesus told us about how the blind couldn't guide the blind, he was leading up to his real message about hypocrites."

"Hypocrites are people who don't practice what they preach. Right?"

Grandfather scratched his head.

"Well, not exactly. No one, including me, always practices what he preaches. No one does what's right all the time. Your definition would make everyone a hypocrite. I think it's better to say that a hypocrite is someone who tells other people what they need to do, and makes them think that he's living that way, while all the time he's deliberately breaking his own rules."

"All right. But what was Jesus' point?"

"It relates to something Jobal heard Jesus say once. The

saying was something like 'Not everyone who seems religious is really a good person.' Does that help?"

"I think so," I said after considering for a moment. "Jesus is telling us something we already know. He's reminding us that some people are liars. Just as people can lie about money, or what they did last week, they can also lie when they act religious. They can pray out loud, pretend to be good, wear their best clothes to worship, and still be as selfish as the worst pagan."

Grandfather nodded in agreement.

"But, Grandfather," I said, "I've heard you and John the Baptist and other prophets say the very same thing."

"So? What else do you expect us to do? Prophets have to keep repeating one another since most people don't ever listen to what they had to say the first time."

Looking off into the distance, Grandfather stopped talking and stared at the nearby mountains. I could tell that he was thinking because his lips parted slightly. His jaw must relax when he's in thought.

I still didn't want to do my chores for the evening. I wanted to feel holy like my grandfather so I too stared at the mountains. I tried to make my face look like I was thinking about something important. Although I must admit that I really didn't know what to think about. But at least I wanted my face to look holy.

There was the sound of a crow flying nearby. He croaked out a greeting and flew in search of food. Grandfather looked over at me. I think he could tell what I was doing.

"Joel, I realize that you're a smart boy. And, who knows, someday you may become a prophet. But when you try to act holy, when you try to make other people think that you're better than you really are, don't you see that you're on your way to being one of the hypocrites that Jesus talked about? Don't start fooling yourself about being holy. God can always tell when you're putting on an act."

I hadn't thought of that. And it wasn't so much that I was trying to show off (although that was part of it) as that I wanted to put off doing my chores. I said I was sorry.

"That's all right. You're still a good boy. But even the best of boys can't sit around and do nothing. Get your work done."

"Interesting story, Deborah," said my father Luke when he finished reading it.

I said thanks.

"It's different from your other ones though. There's a lot more talk and less action."

I told him that I knew that.

"But when you're writing about a sermon someone gave," I said, "you can't expect it to be exciting, Father. Your gospel has lots of speeches and conversations too. That sort of thing can't be as dramatic as stories where a lot happens. I'll make the next one more lively."

CHAPTER 5

"I f you want a story with a little more action, Deborah," said my father the next day, "try using this passage which tells about Jesus calming a storm. The story comes from Mark's Gospel."

"Are you using the same story in your gospel?"

"Well, yes, the story is the same. But Mark quotes Jesus saying to the disciples, 'Don't you have *any* faith?' I thought that was too sarcastic for Jesus. Because I don't think that that question was exactly what he said when he asked the disciples about their faith, I decided to change the words to what he was more likely to have said. You can see the difference in the story if you compare Mark's story with mine."

"All right. I'll give it a try."

Joseph's Story

(Luke 8:22-25)

My father and I met Jesus on a boat ride. We had been doing some business in Capernaum and needed to sail across the Sea of Galilee when we had finished. We do a lot of walking in our business. Because we spend so much time on our feet, when we get the chance to travel by boat, my father usually pays the extra expense of a voyage.

My name is Joseph. My father Jonathan is a merchant. His business is buying and selling jewelry. He is teaching me the trade. Our work involves traveling around Palestine and Syria. We keep our eyes open for nice pieces of jewelry and will buy, if the price is right. But we make our money by selling what we buy. You just have to make sure that you sell the merchandise for more than what you paid for it.

"There's only one secret to business, Joseph," says my father. "Buy low and sell high."

He always laughs when he says that.

I enjoy the business. We get to handle a lot of beautiful merchandise. But the buying and selling of jewelry can be a dangerous business. Robbers sometimes attack travelers. And you can be sure that if robbers knew about the silver and gold we usually carry, we would be prime targets for

assault. That's why my father and I always carry knives with us. I've never had to use mine, but my father has.

When we travel, we usually try to go with other merchants. Robbers are less likely to attack a large group. The merchants we travel with are all in different types of business. One of our companions, Bartholomew, sells cloth. Most of the material he has is made of wool, but some of his more expensive cloth is colored linen. He has even had silk on some trips. Old Man Ezekial—that's what everyone calls him—sells exotic pottery. You can buy plain pottery jars and pots in any village in Palestine, but Old Man Ezekial only works with glazed, colorful pieces. Ezekial and Bartholomew also take a couple of donkeys with them to carry their merchandise. Finally there's David. He sells cut and uncut stones. We sometimes buy jewels from him so that we can have them mounted into necklaces or bracelets. I don't know where he buys stones, and Father says it's better not to ask. He says that in business there are some times when you're better off not knowing things.

We had been traveling with the regular group in northern Palestine when we sold out our stock in Capernaum. Since it looked like the other merchants would need to spend a couple more weeks on the road, Father decided we would go home. We left the others outside Capernaum and walked the short distance to the waterfront.

The boats of Capernaum were not impressive. Even the biggest was only slightly larger than a fishing boat. It wasn't nearly the size of the ships you can see in real seaports like Joppa. The boat we saw near the beach had only one sail. The mast was centered on the deck. There were boxes and jugs stored in the hold. But the hold was only about one third full.

"I guess this will have to do," said my father. He might have been talking to me, but I can't always tell. He seldom looks at me, even when he means for me to listen.

He began waving and shouting to the captain. When the captain finally looked at us, my father asked if he would take us across. The captain said sure. That was how he made his living.

Once we were on board, Father argued with the captain about how much it should cost. That took about ten minutes. Then he paid our fare. We were the only passengers at the time, so we claimed the spot in the shade of the sail and started waiting to shove off.

After about an hour I could tell that Father was growing impatient. He always likes things to be done in a hurry and hates to wait for anything.

"Hey, Skipper," he called. "When are we shoving off? We've been waiting here for hours."

"Sorry," said the captain from the bow where he was working with his two sailors. "But I really need a few more passengers or a bit more cargo to make it worth my while. As soon as we get a few more people, we'll go."

The captain went back to his work.

"We should ask for our money back," muttered my father under his breath. I could tell that he wanted me to be the only one who heard him. "Maybe we could find another boat."

There wasn't anything in sight except a few fishing boats. But it didn't seem like a good idea to point that out to him.

Father grumbled again. I couldn't hear what he was saying. He often does that sort of thing. My mother has warned me not to bother him when he's in that kind of mood. She could have saved her breath. I know what he's like too.

Since there was nothing else to do except wait, we waited. We stayed in the shade and ate a few figs. In the shade I felt comfortable. I felt like having a nap. But Father only drummed his fingers on the deck.

Pretty soon we saw a small crowd walking down the beach. I was still feeling sleepy but didn't want to be napping when we shoved off. I forced myself to count the people coming towards us. There were thirteen. They all seemed to be younger than my father.

One of the men waved to our skipper.

"Dave, you fat son of a sailor," he called.

The captain waved back. He didn't seem to mind being called fat. Anyway, he was fat.

"How have things been with you, Peter?" said the captain. "I hear that 'Peter' is what you want to be called now. It beats me why 'Simon' wasn't good enough for you."

"Well, it's a long story. I'll tell you about it sometime, if you like. But right now we need a ride across. Got room?"

"Sure thing. See for yourself. Come on." The captain waved for them to come aboard. "And, by the way, if that's the Prophet Jesus with you, I'd like to meet him."

Next thing I knew we were drifting away from shore. The thirteen men had boarded the boat and paid their fare. (Father wondered out loud if they got a group discount.) At first we moved slowly. But as the boat got further from the shore, its speed increased. The little splashes and white foam at the bow made me think of how quickly we were going home. I leaned over the side to get a better view of the waves and water.

"You, boy!" shouted the captain. "Don't lean out so far."

When I shifted my weight back on to the deck, the captain explained that a wave might make me lose my balance. He mentioned that unless I were a very good swimmer—and I'm not, by the way—I would probably drown before the boat could turn around and pick me up.

Even though I was embarrassed to have the captain yell at me, at least he explained why I wasn't supposed to lean over the side. You see, if my father had told me not to lean out, I wouldn't have paid any attention to him. I would have obeyed him right then, but when he wasn't looking, I would have leaned out again. My father tells me not to do all sorts of things. But he almost never gives a reason for not doing something. And when he does give a reason, it's usually some made-up reason, like my hair will fall out or my eyes will cross. You get the idea. Those made-up reasons used to scare me when I was a little boy, but now they just sound ridiculous.

It's even getting to the point where I don't believe much of what my father says. I wish that wasn't the case. Father is quite good in business. But Father has told me, and everyone else he knows, so many whoppers that I don't know when to believe him.

Anyway, if my father had told me to quit leaning out over the side, I probably would have leaned out as soon as he wasn't looking at me. Then I would have fallen into the water and drowned. I never would have seen my mother and friends again.

Since I wasn't looking over the side, I decided to study the passengers. It was easy to tell who was the leader of the group. Whenever he wanted to talk, everyone else got quiet. I heard someone call him "Jesus." He must have been that prophet the captain had mentioned.

"Who is this Jesus person?" I asked my father. No one could hear us talking. "Have you ever heard of him?"

"He's some kind of prophet or something. I've heard that some people think he may be the Messiah. It's rubbish, of course. The Messiah is going to be someone important. Just look at that fellow! Look at his clothes and the jokers around him! Does he look like someone important? This Jesus is really just a glorified storyteller. He tells stories to people."

"What does he talk about?"

"How should I know? Anyway, it's not important. I've got enough on my mind as it is without wasting time listening to crackpots talk about things they don't know about. Let the priests and the prophets take care of the religion business, and I'll take care of my business."

My father says that sort of thing when he doesn't think the topic is worth additional conversation. I figured he was either going to lose his temper or start to ignore me, so I got quiet.

Jesus must have been tired. Right after he spoke for a few minutes with the captain, he went below the deck into the hold for a nap. I was wondering about taking a nap myself, but the wind was beginning to pick up. The boat was rocking a little too much for my stomach.

I looked up into the sky and could see dark clouds forming to the north in the mountains. As I watched the clouds billowing up during the next ten minutes, I realized that they were also spreading over the Sea of Galilee. The wind was blowing faster now and the boat was moving rapidly through the water. I felt a little queasy.

I was about to tell my father that a storm was brewing, but then I saw what he was doing. His hand was in his money bag. He counts with his hand inside the pouch so that strangers can't see how much he has. His fingers can tell the difference between the various coins even without his eyes seeing them. He doesn't like being disturbed when he's counting. I didn't bother him.

Soon the sky was totally overcast. The ropes on the sail were taut. I could taste the fresh spray from the water hitting my face. The waves were definitely bigger. You could feel the boat shiver when a wave crashed into the side.

"What's going on here?" asked my father as spray sprinkled his face. He took his hand out of his money bag.

No one answered him. The captain and two sailors were too busy tying or untying ropes. The passengers just looked scared.

Suddenly it started raining. What a rain it was! It hurt my face. We covered our eyes so that they wouldn't get stung. The waves were even bigger than before. It felt like the boat was bouncing on the water just the way a ball bounces on the street.

I was scared. When my father noticed how scared I was, he stumbled over to me and put his arm around my shoulder. I was surprised. He doesn't do that often.

"Don't worry, Joseph." He had to shout for me to hear. "We're not going to die. The captain knows what he's doing."

My father tried to say that in a brave voice, but I could tell that he was frightened too. I wanted to believe him. Looking around the boat, everyone else seemed frightened as well. The captain's face was as white as the sail. Then I noticed Jesus. He was still sleeping!

Since he was below in the hold with the cargo, the deck had been a roof and kept the rain off him. Apparently his friends must have seen him at the same time I did because a couple of them pointed to where he was sleeping. He didn't even know about the storm. I couldn't hear what they said to one another.

Things kept getting worse. The wind blowing across the boat almost sounded like an animal howling. Chunks of hail came down with the rain and ricocheted on the deck. The tops of the waves were splashing into the boat. Each time a wave crashed over us, there was a little more water in the hold. I realized that we were filling with water. If the boat took on much more water, we were going to sink.

I was too scared to cry now. My stomach felt tight and my legs couldn't move. I wished I could be home with my mother.

The friends of Jesus stood over by him.

"Master, master," they shouted. "We're sinking."

What they expected Jesus to do, I don't know.

But Jesus got up and walked to the side of the boat. He stretched his arms out over the water. It looked like he was praying. The scene was dramatic. The boat bouncing up and down in the waves, the rain falling, and Jesus holding his arms out over the waves.

Within a minute the storm began to lessen. The rain stopped suddenly. In five more minutes the waves no longer had whitecaps. The wind had turned into a breeze.

Jesus turned towards his friends.

"Where was your faith?" he asked them.

No one answered him. He walked back to the spot where

he had been taking a nap. He lay down and, I suppose, went back to sleep again. He really must have been tired.

One of his friends said, "What kind of man is he? Even the winds and waves obey him."

There was enough breeze for the boat to sail at a steady speed across the sea. We were all pretty quiet. No one wanted to make noise and wake Jesus up. It wasn't long before we reached the other side.

Jesus woke up and stretched when we arrived at the dock. He and his friends were just stepping off when my father ran over to him.

"Master," he said. "Thank you for saving my life. You must have been sent from God. Please take some of this money as a payment for what you did."

I had never heard my father offer to give money to anyone. He must really have been scared during the storm. One of Jesus' friends started to take the money and put it into the money bag he was carrying, but Jesus waved him aside.

Because I was trying to step off the boat at this time, I couldn't hear everything that was said. Jesus was saying something like he didn't charge people for his help. I think Jesus might also have asked my father if he was sure that his life had been saved. I wish I could have heard what he really said.

Jesus and his friends went off in another direction. We left the port and headed for home. After an hour of walking, I was curious about why my father hadn't said a word to me.

"What did he say to you, Father? What was that about whether you really had been saved?"

"Beats me, Joe."

After another half hour of silent walking we were almost home. Only another couple of hours to go. I asked another question.

"What sort of person is this Jesus?"

"How should I know?" He said without looking at me. "Just what's gotten into you, boy? Let the priests and the prophets take care of the religion business, and I'll take care of my business. Don't worry about things you don't need to know about."

We walked the rest of the way home in silence.

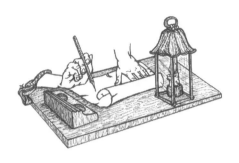

CHAPTER 6

Since my father was following Mark's Gospel in the story of the storm and the next few events in Jesus' life without making many changes, I used the passage which came right after the last one for my next story. It told about a man who had been possessed by a demon.

To say that a person is "possessed by a demon" means that the person is ill in such a way that he can't think properly. The person himself is not in control of what he does. Now some people say that a demon, which is also called an evil spirit, lives inside the person. But other people say that the phrase "possessed by a demon" is just a way of talking to describe something we can't explain. It doesn't really have to mean that there is someone else living inside the person. Just like a person can be sick in his stomach, another person can be sick in his brain. One kind of sickness makes you hurt. The other kind doesn't let you act like other people.

Samuel's Story

(Luke 8:26-39)

My name is Samuel. My family and I live in the Gerasene region of Palestine, on the the south side of the Sea of Galilee. We are poor.

Only a few years ago we had not been poor. But one winter when I was about six, my father came down with a bad cold. No one in the family thought very much about it at the time. He coughed a lot, but everyone does that when they're sick. Still Daddy never really got over the cold. And some of the sickness must have gone down from his head into his legs. In fact soon after he got sick, he starting having trouble walking. Within a year he couldn't walk at all. Because we are so poor, he must go everyday to the synagogue or marketplace and beg for money. I wish he could be well like he used to be.

My mother works as a maid. She cooks, washes clothes, and does other household work for wealthy people in the town. She has to work very hard. She used to be a smiling, nice-looking woman. Now all the work is wearing her down. Her smiles don't come as often as they did when Daddy was well. She is tired most of the time she's at home. She's cross more often too. Because she is always out working or tired, she makes my older sister Ester look after us younger children.

Ester does not do a good job of looking after us. She is seventeen and as lazy as they come. That wouldn't be bad by itself, but she is also mean to us. She doesn't like us younger children. In the morning, after Daddy has gone off to beg and Mother has left for her jobs, Ester gives the rest of us children a piece of bread and tells us to get lost. We're not supposed to go back home until right before our parents return.

Men from the town come over to see Ester during the day. They come, one at a time, and stay for a little bit and then go away. I don't know most of them. If one of us younger children gets sick or hungry and needs to come home during the day, Ester beats him or her with one of her belts and says to go away. She doesn't want anyone at home when people come to visit her.

Often the four of us younger kids have thought of telling Mother about how bad Ester is. But Ester has warned us. If we ever tell on her, if we even suggest that she isn't a responsible babysitter, she'll make us wish that we had never been born. That's just the way she has said it, "You'll wish that you had never been born."

It's a funny thing to say. It's a funny thing because there already have been lots of times that I wished that I hadn't been born. But, since I've already been born, and since I know how spiteful Ester can be, I keep my mouth shut.

I don't know what my two little sisters do during the day, but my brother and I spend our time hanging around the city. We play with some of the other boys from our neighborhood. Most of the time we go outside the town. We have to do that since the merchants don't like us running down the streets and disturbing their customers. They usually try to chase us away themselves, but they sometimes have called one of the policemen to get rid of us. I've been hit more than once by the policeman or one of the merchants with their sticks.

We still stay in the town on some days though. On days like this we beg, or get into fights with kids from other neighborhoods, or try to steal things from the markets. I can remember back to the time before Daddy got sick. We were told that things like that were wrong. I suppose it's still wrong for us healthy boys to beg when there are sick people who need the money more. I also guess that it's not really fair for four or five of us boys to beat up one kid from another neighborhood. And I can remember being told that it's wrong to steal things.

But what's the point of being good? I used to think a lot about being good. I can remember when I was little how Mother told us about how important it was to do the right things. But what difference does it make now? There were times when I promised God I would be good if he would make Daddy get well again. But it never happened. God must not have been listening. He probably doesn't care a bit about those of us who are poor around here. So, I ask you, why should I bother being nice to anyone? No one is ever nice to me.

I don't know though. Maybe if someone, even one person, treated me right, things would change. But that's the kind of thing that won't ever happen. You hear stories about that kind of thing, but it really doesn't happen in the real world. All I have to do is look at my vicious sister, my crippled father, my exhausted mother, and then at all the proud, healthy people in town, and I wonder what would even be the point of trying to be different.

When the boys from my neighborhood play outside the city, we have lots of fun. There are all kinds of games that we play. We run races and wrestle and throw rocks. We have other games too. Sometimes we pretend like we're soldiers and have a war. And on a few occasions we pretend like we're rich people in town and imagine how we would pay back the people who have been mean to us. I would like to make them have to beg and go hungry. But these are only games.

There have been some times when we've done bad things outside the town. There used to be this crazy man who lived by the graveyard. He was something to see. He didn't wear any clothes. His hair went down to his waist, and it was matted and filthy with dirt. If you got close to him, you could see the bugs in his hair and beard. Spit would slobber out of his mouth. He even slept on the graves.

Can you blame us for being mean to him? We used to

hide out in the bushes and watch him. He would sing and talk to himself. On days when it was cloudy or when it was getting dark, he would dance around by the graves, singing to himself. Sometimes, when we were hiding, we threw rocks at him. We'd laugh at him when he tried to figure out where the stones were coming from. But when he'd see us and come running with rocks of his own, we'd run away.

One day after he had beaten up two of my friends that he'd caught, the people of the town decided that enough was enough. They wanted to lock him into chains. After capturing him with fishing nets, of all things, they fastened the chains to his arms and legs and were beginning to drag him away when he started screaming. He was shaking his arms and legs like they were on fire.

I felt sorry for him. We had been throwing rocks at him before he caught the two boys. No one liked him and now he was going to locked up in the jail. But then one of the chains snapped. I don't know how a man could have broken the metal, but he did.

He swung the broken chain over his head. It went through the air so fast that you could hear the metal whistling. While the men ran back to the town, he ran into the desert country towards the east. In a few days though, he was back sleeping and living in the graveyard. The chains were gone. He had smashed them to bits on the rocks, I guess.

You might have noticed that I said that there "used to be this crazy man." That's true. He isn't crazy anymore though. Something weird happened to him.

One afternoon a few months after he had broken out of the chains, we were watching him from one of the hills near the Sea of Galilee. We were bored. (You can tell there isn't much to do where I live.) When we saw that a boat was going to land nearby, we left Crazy Jacob—that was his name—and went down to look at the boat. About a dozen men left the boat and started down the road towards the south. We realized this meant that they would have to walk near Crazy Jacob. We went back up the hill to watch what was going to happen.

Jacob had been dancing among the graves that afternoon. Suddenly he stopped and sniffed the air. It was just like what an animal would do. Then he began to howl like a dog. When he saw the men come into view on the road, he ran towards them screaming. He wasn't saying any words. He was just screaming.

Several of the men were frightened, but no one ran back. Crazy Jacob must not have expected this. When they didn't run from him, he stopped and looked them over. He must have recognized one of them.

"What is there between you and me, Jesus?" he shouted. I could see that he was shaking. "Please, don't hurt me."

The man who was named Jesus stood in the front of the group. It didn't look to me that Jesus was hurting Jacob at all. The two men stood there, looking at one another. We boys began moving closer to hear better.

"What is your name?" asked Jesus. He was calm.

"Legion."

That Crazy Jacob was off his rocker all right. Everyone knew his name was Jacob. And "Legion" isn't even a person's name at all. It's a word that means a large group of Roman soldiers, about six thousand men, I think.

As we moved closer, we couldn't hear everything that Jesus and Jacob said. There was something about Jacob not wanting to go to a pit and him asking a question about a herd of pigs that was nearby. Jesus answered the question with a nod of his head. Jacob, who was pointing at the pigs, fell over with a scream.

I guess the pigs were scared by the scream. They went

into a panic. Within a few minutes they were stampeding over the hillside and heading towards a cliff that overlooked the sea. Still squealing and snorting, they began to go over the side into the water. Lots of them got drowned.

While this was going on, we decided not to stick around. We went back to town with the pig herders. We told everyone about what had happened. We told about how demons must have come out of Crazy Jacob and flown over in the air to where the pigs were and made them go crazy. One of the pig herders said that he had seen the demons flying in the air. That seemed to be what the people in the town wanted to hear, so pretty soon we all were saying the same thing. The town leaders decided to hold an emergency meeting. They didn't want anyone like Jesus causing trouble around our town.

Nathan, one of the rich shopkeepers, made a speech.

"Friends," he shouted. (I had never heard him call anyone a friend before or since, but that was how he started.) "Friends, do we want troublemakers hanging around here?"

I wasn't sure whom Nathan had in mind. Was he talking about us? Or Crazy Jacob? Or Jesus?

We found out in a second or two.

"If this Jesus is the same one we've heard stories about," he continued, "is he the kind of person to have here with us? I say no. We've heard stories about this Jesus person. He causes trouble. He changes things. Do we really want our lives changed?"

Well, I wouldn't have minded my life being changed. I would like to have Ester exchanged for someone else, and it would be good to have Daddy work again. I was ready for a change. But no one was asking me.

"Jesus will only bring us trouble," he said. "We really ought to figure out some way to get rid of him."

The townspeople agreed with Nathan and they kept talking into the night. Three spies were sent out to see if Jesus had left the area. But they saw that Jesus and his friends were camped out near the hill where they had met Jacob. By the next morning the elders had decided on a plan. Since Jesus seemed to have some sort of magic power, no one wanted to risk anything by being rude. The first plan was to ask him politely to go back home. If that didn't work, they would offer him some money to leave. If that didn't work, they would need to make another plan.

Almost the whole town walked out to the place where Jesus was camped. When we got there, we were surprised to see Crazy Jacob sitting next to Jesus. But Jacob didn't look crazy any more. He was wearing clothes. He had bathed, and somebody must have cut the mats out of his hair. The main difference, though, was in his eyes. He looked normal. I was shocked. It just wasn't normal.

"That's the Prophet Jesus all right," someone whispered to Nathan. This man pointed at the person Jacob had called Jesus. I figured he must be famous, but I had never heard of him.

"Mighty sir," Nathan called out as we approached Jesus. "We realize that you are a great prophet sent from God. How else could anyone do the things you do?"

Nathan went on buttering Jesus up with his speech for a few minutes. The long and short of it was that our town thought that Jesus could better serve God by going to some other town. Nathan said that there were plenty of places more sinful than our town and that Jesus could probably get a better response by working there.

I guess Nathan and the others must have convinced Jesus with that line of thinking because Jesus and his friends decided that they would go back north. Most people were relieved. Some looked happy. I saw Ester look at one of her men friends and smile.

As Jesus and his friends left the hillside and walked back to the shore, Jacob ran towards them.

"Wait!" he said. "Oh, please, take me with you."

Crazy Jacob wanted to go with Jesus. I couldn't blame him. Who in his right mind would want to stay here with us? But Jesus didn't think that was a good idea. He told Jacob to stay here.

"Return to your own place," said Jesus. "Show to others what God has done for you."

That was that. Jesus left in a boat and we haven't seen him again.

But there has been at least one difference in life around here. Jacob is an entirely different person. He talks to people in the town and tells them about how good God is. A lot of people make fun of him. Some of them have said that he's as crazy as ever. But I don't believe it.

For one thing he has started to make friends with us boys. Even though we used to throw rocks at him when he was crazy, he's trying to be friends. I can't get over that.

CHAPTER 7

O ver the next weeks my father Luke continued working on his gospel. Most of the time he took stories about Jesus from Mark, but at other times he used material which Mark hadn't included. And, even though he followed Mark's order in the overall story of Jesus' life, he almost always rephrased what Mark had written.

After reading my father's retelling of the events from Jesus' life, I started to notice patterns in how my father rephrased the stories from Mark. He regularly made changes to emphasize what women were doing or how poor people were of special concern to God. Mark had also been more critical about Peter and the other disciples than my father was. If you read the stories about Jesus and the disciples as they're described in the Gospel According to Luke and then compare them to the ones in the other gospels, you'll see that difference.

It wasn't often that my father came across a story about Jesus which specifically mentioned children. So when I found out that he was using one from Mark, I knew I would want to use it too.

Eve's Story

(Luke 8:40-56)

My father is a very important man. He is the leader of our town's synagogue. His name is Jairus.

My own name is Eve. I am my parents' only child. Before I was born my parents expected to have a lot of children. But since my birth they haven't had any more. At first they were disappointed not to have an Adam (so they could have their own Adam and Eve), and an Abraham and a Sarah, and who knows how many others. But things didn't work out that way.

Now they tell me that they're glad they only have me. My mother says that they can look after me alone better than if I had five or six brothers and sisters. I don't mind being an only child. But I know it is hard sometimes on my mother and father not having more children.

In our culture it is important to have lots of children. For one reason, a husband and wife want to have children so that their children will grow up and look after their parents when their father and mother are too old to work. In addition, since we say that children are a blessing from God, if you don't have children that means that God is not blessing you. In fact, if a wife doesn't have a lot of children, some people think that God is punishing her. If God really loved her, these people say, she would have a large family. (But I don't believe what those people say because I don't think that God works that way.)

Women are expected to get married when they're young and have a lot of kids. I'm twelve now and could be married within the next couple of years. But my parents would first need to find someone they would like for me to marry. My parents will choose a husband for me. They have to make the choice about whom I will marry. That isn't a choice girls get to make. Still, my parents have promised that I will get to meet my future husband before we get married. They have even said that if I don't like him, I won't have to marry him. That is something they don't have to do. In fact, in our culture sometimes girls don't get to meet their future husbands until the day of the wedding. But by then, it's too late to say no if you don't like him.

I want to have seven children once I get married. But that's not because I think God would be rewarding me for being good. Instead it's because I want to find out what life is like with a big family. Right now most people say it's better to have boy babies rather than girl babies. But I think I would like a mix.

Since my father is the leader of our synagogue, he is always interested in any religious news. He visits Jerusalem several times each year and goes out to hear any prophets or rabbis who are passing near our town.

The leader of a synagogue is not like a priest or a prophet. He is in charge of the worship that we do in the synagogue. He also does some of the teaching and is probably closest to being a rabbi, who is also a teacher. But a rabbi, who can have almost any kind of job, doesn't always act as the leader of a synagogue.

It was a year or so ago that my father first heard anything about the prophet Jesus.

"I talked with some travelers today," he said one evening. (He tells my mother and me everything.) "They mentioned hearing a new prophet. A Jesus from Nazareth. They were quite impressed by him. He gave a short sermon and told a few stories. They said he also performed miracles. Not in front of them, of course, but the day before—"

"What are miracles, Father?" I asked. He doesn't mind being interrupted with serious questions. "You've mentioned miracles before, but the word is used in a lot of different ways."

He thought for a moment.

"A miracle is something that doesn't happen very often. It's an event which normally doesn't occur. Now this Jesus—"

"You mean it's like magic?"

"No, not at all," he said. He frowned. "A miracle isn't a bit like magic. Most magic is only a set of tricks. Men learn to do a few clever things with their fingers, and they get you to think that they're making things disappear or making them appear out of thin air. It's just entertainment. There's nothing really bad about it as long as it's done for show. But a miracle is something different. God is the one who performs miracles, even though he uses people along the way. Now this Jesus—"

"But if there's nothing really bad about magic, why do our Scriptures tell us that it is evil?"

"That's because there are two types of magic. One type is the tricks you see people do in the marketplace. I watch them myself sometimes. But there's another type of magic where people make agreements with the demons to know the future, or to have someone killed, or to do something else they're not supposed to. I don't think that this kind of magic exists anywhere but inside people's heads. But there are some people who think that you really can make deals with evil spirits."

I wasn't following all that, and, since he still hadn't answered my question, I asked, "Can you give me an example of a miracle?"

"A miracle would be a sick person getting well," he said.

"But sick people get well all the time. I don't see what's so special about that."

"Eve's right," said my mother. She hadn't said anything yet. "Sick people often get well, but they sometimes die. I don't see that you're answering her question."

Mother had him there. My father thought for a minute.

He knew that we weren't going to let him go on with the news about Jesus the prophet until he answered my question.

"Let's try again," he said. "A miracle would be someone getting well when he has something wrong with him that doesn't normally get better on its own. Think about the blind man who begs in the marketplace or in front of the synagogue. People who are born blind don't ever learn to see. If that blind man were to be healed, if he came to see, that would be a miracle."

My mother nodded at him. After this interruption about miracles, my father went back to his story about Jesus. Even though none of the travelers had seen any miracles, they had heard about Jesus healing various people: a paralyzed man, a woman with a fever, a man possessed by demons, and so on.

We were silent when he finished. Then my mother spoke again.

"What else does he do, Jairus?"

"He does a lot of things, dear. But I'm more interested in what he says. He teaches by telling parables. Sometimes these parables are stories, and sometimes they are simple sentences which make a picture form in your mind.

"For example, he said that no one lights a lamp and then hides it under a basket. Well, of course. Putting a shining light inside a basket doesn't make any sense. No one would be able to see the light. But this is a parable. The trick to understanding the parable is figuring out that he isn't talking about lamps and baskets at all. He's talking about how our lives need to show what we believe. If you say that you love God, or love other people, that love needs to show in your life. You can't keep it a secret. In fact, if it doesn't show, it must be that it doesn't even exist."

He was quiet for a minute or so. My mother and I looked at him. We knew he was about to say something else.

"I wish I could make my points as neatly when I speak

at the synagogue. But my ideas just don't come out the way they should."

That was true. My father is a wonderful man, but I am not blind to the areas where he could improve. (My mother says the same thing.) When he leads the worship in the synagogue, he reads the Scriptures beautifully. He has a wonderful voice for leading us when we chant the psalms. It makes me feel that I am really worshipping God when we sing. But when my father tries to explain the passages from the Scriptures, I can't understand him. I even hear the grownups saying the same thing. From what my father was saying, he must know that he doesn't always keep our attention in the synagogue when he's trying to explain things to us. But it didn't seem proper to agree with him at the dinner table.

Off and on for the next few weeks, he talked about Jesus. More travelers passed through our town and had news of Jesus. Father had spoken with some of his friends about a group walking out to hear Jesus speak someday when he was in the area.

Then we heard that Jesus was coming to our town. I don't know if he meant to stay here or whether he was on his way to Jerusalem, but Father didn't intend to miss him.

I was getting excited about hearing Jesus too, but then I got sick. It started off with a fever. No one else in the family was ill. I began throwing up and didn't want to eat anything. Because I wasn't eating, I was too weak to walk. My mother needed some help looking after me, so she wrote a letter to some of my father's relatives and asked for help.

On the day Jesus arrived, I was sicker than ever before. I felt so bad that I passed out in the morning. Since I was in bed, I didn't fall onto anything and hurt myself. Instead I just stopped being aware of what was happening around me. I was so tired of throwing up, and having a bad taste in my mouth, and being hot, and feeling thirsty that I was

glad to be going to sleep. But I never really went to sleep. It just felt like I was going to. It's like one of the nights when you're almost asleep but part of you is still a little awake. You're not thinking clearly, and you feel like you could wake up if you wanted to, but you don't want to.

I felt very relaxed. Even though I could feel my stomach hurting, it was as if the stomach hurting wasn't mine. I went into a dream where the stomach-ache belonged to a sick girl in my bed and I was somebody else who was invisible floating near the ceiling as I watched her. There were worried-looking people in the room sitting by her.

There were other strange dreams I had that day. Of course, I wonder now whether I've gotten my dreams confused with what was happening outside our house. (Later on my parents told me about what had happened.) I have to admit that everything from that day is still all jumbled in my memory.

In the first dream I was floating around the ceiling and looking at a sick girl on my bed. Her face was very pale. My father was sitting at the side of the bed holding this girl's hand. I wondered why he wasn't out listening to the prophet Jesus. That was what he had planned to do that day. My mother was standing next to him and crying.

"My poor baby," she was saying. "She's still so young."

Father wasn't saying anything, but I could see the tears rolling down his face. All of our visiting relatives were spread throughout the house. They felt sorry for my father, mother, and the little girl in the bed. They were whispering things like "She hasn't got much longer" and "It's such a shame they couldn't have had more children."

Then, for a moment, my father's face brightened. He must have had an idea. He stood up and left the room.

Once out of the room, he was telling our relatives what he had in mind. Someone told him that he needed to face facts. Someone else warned him about making a fool of himself. I wondered what he had in mind. He left the house in a hurry.

I couldn't have seen this next part of the dream so someone must have told me about it. My father ran through the streets until he came to a crowd which surrounded the prophet Jesus. Father forced his way through until he came to Jesus. Then, because he was exhausted from the run and from worrying about me, he fell at Jesus' feet.

"Please, sir," he said. "Please save my daughter. She's dying."

Jesus reached down and helped him to his feet. Jesus said something to him, and a group of men and women started walking to our house. Their trip was interrupted by a sick woman who asked for something from Jesus, but I don't know what it was. Somebody touched him, I think.

One of my cousins must have decided that the little girl on the bed was as good as dead. He went to my father in the street and spoke loud enough for everyone else in the crowd to hear.

"Your daughter is dead," he said, assuming that the sick girl in my bed had already died, I suppose. "There's no need to trouble the teacher."

My father covered his face with his hands. Jesus and the others with him just kept on walking to our house.

Before the group entered our house, they could hear our relatives sobbing and groaning. (In our culture you're supposed to make a lot of noise when you're in grief.) Everyone must have thought that the little girl was dead.

Jesus and a few of his friends came into the room where I was. (Remember that in this dream of mine that I'm describing now, I'm still floating around up near the ceiling, watching all this.) They crowded into the room with my relatives. Jesus looked at the girl on the bed and said that there wasn't any need to cry.

"She's not dead. She's only sleeping."

Our relatives didn't like that at all. One of my cousins said, "Go back to your carpenter's shop. You can't even tell when someone is dead. You know about wood not medicine."

My Uncle Abram said sarcastically, "Of course, she's asleep. She's sleeping just the same way the first Eve is sleeping."

A few people thought that was really funny. I could hear them laughing.

One of Jesus' friends got angry at that. His face started turning red. Jesus must have been upset too, but he didn't show it in his face. Still he made everyone leave the room except three of his friends and my mother and father. I guess he didn't see me floating around the ceiling looking at the girl on the bed.

Then I went into another dream. This time I was the little girl on the bed. I could see five men and one woman looking at me. Jesus was holding my hand and calling my name. But all the time I felt like I was falling.

Now the funny thing about all this is that I wasn't scared. I dream about falling a lot. Especially right when I'm drifting off to sleep. Sometimes it makes me wake up all nervous and sweaty. But this time I dreamed I was falling and I wasn't afraid. I wasn't falling very fast, but I could tell I was moving. Things were peaceful and I was sure that nothing bad was going to happen to me.

It seemed like I had gone over the edge of a cliff. Of course, that sounds scary to you reading about this. But to me at the time, it seemed very natural. I was falling through the air, but, because I wasn't falling that fast, I wasn't really frightened. The thought that I would probably die when I landed at the bottom of the cliff didn't bother me. I had been sick for so many days that I almost felt happy to think that I would never be sick again.

I wondered what it was going to be like never to grow up. I wasn't going to get old. I wasn't going to have to do housework for the rest of my life. I wasn't going to have to put up with people I couldn't stand. I wouldn't have to suffer pain or sickness or grief.

Jesus was still holding my hand.

Then I began to feel sad. If I died, my parents would miss me terribly. I could see the tears on my father's face. I could hear my mother's breathing. My friends would miss me too. I also realized that if I didn't grow up, I would miss out on what it's like to be a woman, to be in charge of your own life. I thought of how I would never be able to have the large family that I had dreamed about for so long.

"Wake up, little girl. Wake up, Eve."

It was Jesus talking to me.

In my dream I stopped falling. It was like I was floating again, not going down but still not going up. Then I started moving up. As fast as I had fallen in my dream, I was now floating upwards. I could see to the top of the cliff.

It reminded me a little of what it's like to go swimming in deep water and opening your eyes as you move towards

the surface. You see the top of the water as you get closer to it. And then, almost before you know it, you're out of the water.

I was so used to floating upwards in my dream that when I awakened from it, I sat right up in bed. My mother grabbed hold of my father's arm. I could see her eyes opening wide. I felt so much better.

My father and mother were shocked. They didn't say anything. The next thing I knew they were laughing and crying and hugging me. I felt hungry and thirsty.

"Give her something to eat," Jesus said.

They gave me some chicken soup and bread. While my parents fed me, Jesus told my parents not to tell anyone about what had happened.

I couldn't figure out why he said such a thing. Did he really think you could keep this sort of thing secret? Or was he just trying to get out of town before the crowds surrounded him again? Could it have been that he was afraid that the story would be exaggerated if too many people heard about it? I don't know.

After we sat there for a few minutes, Jesus and his friends left our house. They didn't have any soup or bread. None of our relatives had anything to say to them when they left.

My mother and father then talked over what had happened. Because I was still so sleepy, I'm sure that part of my dreams got mixed in with their stories. But I do remember the dream about falling. Later on my parents told me that everyone dreams about falling and that I don't need to get upset about it. They told me that it isn't true that you will die if you're dreaming of falling off a cliff and then dream of hitting the bottom. That's just the way it feels. Well, that's how it feels to me anyway.

Still there are times when I wonder what would have happened if I had actually fallen to the bottom of the cliff in my dream. Sometimes, when I'm depressed or sick, or mad at one of my friends, I wish that Jesus hadn't called me back.

On the other hand, those feelings don't last very long.

There must be some reason why God made me. I don't know what it is. Maybe I will be a mother someday and have seven kids like I talked about. Maybe I'll have only one. It could be that I'll do something else important one day. Who knows?

"Deborah, Deborah," my father Luke called to me. He had finished reading this story about Eve. I was cleaning things in the kitchen after dinner.

"Yes, Father," I said as I walked into the room.

"I liked your story."

"Thanks."

"I wondered about some of the things you said."

"Uh-huh."

"I noticed that the girl was an only child like you." He looked at me, but I looked down at the floor. "Do you also want to have seven children?"

"I don't know. Sometimes I do, and sometimes I don't."

He nodded.

"You also mentioned that Eve would be at the age to get married soon. You know that you're about the same age."

I nodded.

"Do you want me to start looking for a husband for you? There are some families here in town who might like to have one of their sons marry you." He paused. "But you're still very young."

We talked about that. I said that was true. Father promised that he wouldn't start looking for my husband for a few more years. I thought that I would want to wait until I was older. Even being sixteen or seventeen seems young to get married.

But more important than waiting for a few years before he started looking for a husband for me, my father promised that I would get to meet the man who was seriously interested in becoming my husband. My father would let me say no if I didn't like him. My father said that this was only fair.

I thought so too. It's a strange world we live in when most young men and young women don't have any choice about whom they will marry. But that's just the way things have always been.

CHAPTER 8

"Deborah," my father called. "What did you want to tell me earlier today?"

I had been working in another room, reading over what he had written in his gospel that week, checking spelling and making sure that he hadn't left out any words. Since I need something to help me concentrate when I do this, I was slowly reading everything aloud. Everybody I know in town, and that includes the adults too, reads things aloud. It makes you pay attention to what's on the page. When I do this kind of reading, I go into another room so that I won't disturb him.

"An idea occurred to me a few days ago," I said as I came into the room. "I was thinking how it's a lot easier for grownups to understand your writing than it is for children."

"Well, yes, that's true. But it's always easier for adults to read things. I don't understand why you feel you need to tell me that. Is there something else on your mind?"

"I wanted to tell you because it makes what I'm doing seem more important. If your gospel is meant for adults, then is there one meant for children? I'm not sure that there is."

"And should there be?"

"I think so."

"But aren't there some ideas that children just can't understand? That is, depending on their ages, aren't some children just not able to understand certain things?"

"Maybe. But even if there couldn't be a gospel written with only children in mind, there does need to be someone around to explain the strange things in the stories about Jesus."

"Like what?" He had put his pen down and was listening to me.

"Like some of the arguments that Jesus got into. I was trying to write a story that involved an argument that Jesus had with some other people about working on the Sabbath. I couldn't understand why the people around Jesus got so excited about all this."

"You could have asked me."

"I know, but you're not always around, and sometimes you're busy on something. Anyway most kids probably don't have anyone they can ask. There are even grownups in our church who can't explain why Jesus got into arguments about the Sabbath. I know. I've asked them. A few of them just said that Jews love to argue or that the Jews have never really listened to God. But I don't believe that."

"Why's that?" He was more interested in what I was saying.

"For one thing, because Jesus was a Jew. But also because I don't think that the Jews are that different from us. And we get into lots of arguments with one another too. We also worship the same God. I wonder whether some of the people at church, those who say that the Jews don't obey God, just say that because they don't know what else to say. They don't know why Jesus got into debates about the

Sabbath or the Temple or ritual purity—whatever that is—and so they say that the Jews weren't listening to God. I don't like people saying that anyone who disagrees with them is disobeying God. It's a cheap shot. Especially when they can't explain anything about what was going on."

My father looked thoughtfully at me and nodded.

"So you'd like to know why some of the Jewish people were concerned about working on the Sabbath?" he asked.

"Not any more. I asked someone who knew. I know I could have asked you, but instead I asked a Jewish girl in the marketplace about the Sabbath. There are a lot of things I don't understand about the Jewish customs. At first, when she thought that I was hoping to convert her, she didn't want to talk. But once she realized that I was serious about my question, she answered me. She told me that the Jews keep the Sabbath as a holy day, but that there is still discussion among their wise men and rabbis about what they are allowed to do. The Jews all agree that they are not allowed to do any *work* on the Sabbath, but the discussion goes on about the meaning of the word *work.* Just what is this thing *work* that they are not supposed to do?"

"And learning that helped you with a story?"

"Uh-huh," I said. "At least I hope it did. You'll have to decide for yourself. Since Jesus was a Jew, unless you know what was happening with all the other Jews, you can't understand what Jesus was talking about."

Martha's Story

(Luke 13:10-17)

I'm Martha. My friends usually call me "Marty." I live with my parents in a large village in the province of Judea. My grandmother lives with us too. I have a baby brother.

But since he's only a year old, he doesn't do much of anything except eat and sleep.

My father is a stone mason. He does construction work on houses, public buildings, and walls outside of towns. His job involves a lot of different things. He shapes stones with a hammer and chisel, and he also molds bricks. He sets building blocks into place. Sometimes he cements them together. Sometimes the blocks stand on their own without cement. He is a skilled laborer and earns a good living.

His work is hard. It makes him tired. When he is tired, and especially after he's had too much wine, he gets cranky. He yells at me, or my mother, or my grandmother. He has never hit one of us, but he can get very angry. We stay out of his way. My mother tells me that we just have to put up with him.

I guess she's right. He does work hard to give us a place to live and food to eat. And I do love him. There are times when he can tell the nicest stories and play games and be such fun. I just wish he didn't have those bad days.

I spend my days with my mother and grandmother. They are teaching me what I will need to know when I have a home and family of my own. Mother is trying to teach me how to cook. But I'm afraid I'm too absent-minded to be a very good cook. I keep forgetting when I have something in the oven. I'll slip a loaf of bread dough into the oven to bake, go somewhere else to sit down or do some other work, and then forget all about the bread that's supposed to be baking. The smell of the burning bread usually has to reach my nose before I remember what I'm supposed to be doing. I smell the smoke and run to the kitchen. But then it's too late.

Grandmother is making an effort to teach me to sew. I'm much better at sewing than cooking. Grandmother herself is an excellent seamstress. She sews wonderfully. Of course, that's about all she can do nowadays. Her back is

twisted in such a way that she can't stand up straight. She's had this problem from before I was born. For eighteen years, says my father.

Despite her crooked back, she can sew like an angel. (If angels can sew, I guess.) I don't know of anyone who can do more beautiful things with cloth than her. She is also an excellent teacher. She doesn't lose her temper when I ask her to repeat things. She just rephrases her instructions and makes sure that I know what I'm doing. And she has showed me time and time again how to make certain kinds of stitches.

I really like sewing. It seems more rewarding than cooking. You cook something, people eat it, and that's that. But when you sew something, it can last for years. You can even make money by sewing. If you're very good, like Grandmother, sometimes people will hire you to make them clothes. Then you're earning money for doing what you like to do.

My family is very religious, especially my mother. My mother and grandmother make us all go to the synagogue. We are there whenever the doors are open. I agree with my father when he asks them whether we go there too often, but mother and grandmother refuse to argue about this. It's important that my father go since we can't hold a service unless there is a "minyan." Having a minyan means that there are at least ten men present in the congregation. If there's less than ten men, we can't meet. (Women and children don't count towards the ten.)

I don't want you to think that I don't like to worship God. Worshipping God is important, and it's in the synagogue we offer up group prayers and thanks to our God. But there are times when things are just rather boring.

Sometimes I get so sleepy listening to the men talk that I fall asleep on the bench. If I'm next to my grandmother, nothing happens. But if I fall asleep next to my mother, she pinches me and whispers, "Sit up and pay attention."

If the speakers at worship aren't saying anything interesting, why should they get upset if you fall asleep? Now of course some of the visiting teachers and rabbis are very good. They can make it seem that God really is wonderful. But others just make me wish that I was back home in bed. I don't know why Mother gets so upset when I doze off. Whose fault is it anyway when the congregation falls asleep?

There's another thing I don't understand either. That's why the women and men have to sit in different places. The men sit on one side of the synagogue. The women sit on another. There's also something in between the two groups. Sometimes it's a curtain, but usually it's a wall. We can't see them and they can't see us. There was one day while we were at home when I asked my mother if this was right.

"What do mean 'Is it right?'" she asked. "It's what we do, isn't it? How can you even think of, let alone ask, such a question? It is not our place to question the will of God."

I was about to ask her how we could tell what was the will of God, but then we smelled the smoke of burning bread. Mother slapped my hand for letting the bread burn. I couldn't help thinking, though, that she was more upset with my asking questions than with the burning bread. I've burned things in the oven a lot of times and didn't get slapped. I wish I hadn't forgotten about that loaf. I might have learned something about knowing what God wants us to do.

One day my mother told us that a prophet from Galilee was coming to our town and would probably speak in the synagogue. She told my father that we would have to leave early if we wanted to get good seats. My father said all right.

Since I had only heard of one famous prophet in our time, I asked if this was John the Baptist.

My mother looked troubled. There was something she didn't want to talk about.

"I'll tell her," said my father.

I looked at him.

"John the Baptist is dead. Our king Herod Antipas arrested John and had him killed. Herod has sold us out to the Romans all his life and doesn't know the meaning of the word justice. He's as bad, if not worse than his father, Herod the Great. Anyone who stands in his way, or speaks against him, disappears into a prison and soon disappears for good. The king is an absolute—"

"That's enough," said my mother interrupting. Then she

gently put her hand on his arm. "I know how you feel, but we don't want anyone to hear you."

"If a man can't speak the truth in his own house, where can he?" asked my father.

I hadn't seen him look so unhappy in ages. He didn't look mad. He just looked sad. We were quiet for a few minutes. Then my mother spoke to me.

"This is a different prophet, Marty. He was with John the Baptist for a time and then went out on his own. He has his own group of followers now. His name is Jesus."

The next day was the Sabbath. We planned to walk to the synagogue early enough to get good seats. Since we Jews don't work on the Sabbath, Father never has any jobs to finish then and can always go to worship. But this Sabbath he said that he was tired and wanted to worship God at home in prayers and reading by himself. He said that the rest of the family could get by without him. Mother raised her eyebrows at him. She asked him what sort of example he thought he was setting for the family and the community. She was just starting to warm up in the discussion, when he agreed to go with us. My mother almost always wins in a religious discussion.

But their conversation had slowed us down. By the time we walked to the building, Jesus had already started teaching. We had to sit near the back of the crowd. I couldn't see a thing, but I could hear all right. When I tried to move a little to the left so that I could hear better, my mother gave me a pinch.

"Stop fidgeting, girl," she said.

I sat still and prepared myself to be bored. But Jesus turned out to be one of the more interesting rabbis who visit here. He told us a story about a rich man. This rich man had earned a lot of money in the city and one day decided that he was rich enough not to work any more. He was going to move into the country where he would never be bothered

by anyone or anything. Then, on the very night he moved into his mansion in the country to enjoy his riches, the Lord took his life away.

Now there was a story I could understand. Jesus was reminding us that money is not the most important thing in life. Money can't protect you from everything. God is the One we must rely on. I liked the way he taught.

But there were some people who didn't care for what he was saying. Some of the richer women (remember that we can't see the men) didn't look pleased with that parable. I heard one of them whisper, "This is all so simple. I had hoped for something more profound."

I couldn't figure what that lady meant. Are simple things never profound? And, just because you can't understand something, does that make it profound?

When Jesus was leaving, he saw my grandmother. She looked sad. Her back was still bent and twisted. Jesus motioned to her and asked her to come over. The people stared. I felt sorry for her.

When she was almost to him, he streched out his hands, put them upon her shoulders, and spoke.

"Woman, you are healed of your disease."

She straightened up slowly. In all my life I had never seen her stand up straight. She was turned so that we could see her face. Her eyes were getting big and her mouth was open. She began to thank God for what had happened.

I was happy for my grandmother, but she was making a lot of noise. I wondered what our friends would think. Some of Grandmother's friends began thanking God as well. Other people were just looking around at one another.

Then the leader of the synagogue ran forward. He stood in front of the congregation. He waved his hands at us.

"Quiet down," he shouted. "There are six days when you are permitted to work. Those are the days to come here and be healed, not the Sabbath."

Some people agreed with him. "The Sabbath is meant for God, not for work," they said.

That was certainly true. But the leader of the synagogue was only telling part of the story. Grandmother had often come to the building for healing, but nothing had ever happened. The leader's remarks must have upset Jesus because he make a quick reply.

"You hypocrite," he said. "You too work on the Sabbath. And who in this building doesn't feed and water his animals on the Sabbath?"

Now this debate about what to do on the Sabbath may seem strange to Gentiles, that is, people who are not Jews. But the Sabbath is a holy day, and we are not supposed to work on it. Still there is a problem our holy men have. That's figuring out what sort of things count as work and which don't. Not long ago there were two great Jewish teachers who talked a lot about this sort of thing. Rabbi

Hillel and Rabbi Shammai had many debates about the same topic. Even I had heard some of this discussion before. I guessed that the congregation would start it over again now.

"This daughter of Abraham," Jesus continued, "has suffered for many years now. Yet you tell me that it isn't right to heal her on the Sabbath."

The leader of the synagogue was about to reply, but he looked around the congregation. The people clearly sided with Jesus. Jesus' view seemed closer to Rabbi Hillel, who always was the more popular teacher. The leader of the synagogue sat down. Jesus made the congregation quiet down. He told another parable.

In the parable he compared the kingdom of God with a mustard seed. Just as a mustard seed is one of the smallest seeds and yet grows into a large tree, so also the kingdom of God starts out small and then grows.

On the way home my mother and father were quiet. My grandmother wasn't walking with us. She had gone off to see two of her friends.

"Well, what do you think?" Father asked my mother.

"I don't know," she said. "Certainly this is a miracle."

"Yes," he said. "And I never thought I would live to see one. You hear stories about how holy men can heal people, but I've had my doubts."

My mother was about to say something to him, but he went on quickly. He kept his voice low.

"Do you know what I wonder?"

"What?"

"Do you think this Jesus might be the one who drives the Romans out of Israel? Do you think he can free us from that traitor Herod Antipas? Certainly the people are behind him. You could tell that today from the reaction in the synagogue. He could be our leader, maybe even our king, in a great war."

"I don't know," she said, also keeping her voice low.

"The Messiah, or a messiah, might do that. But Jesus doesn't seem the type. I think he's more like one of the prophets than like one of the kings. The prophets sometimes healed. The kings did other things."

When Grandmother returned, she gave me a sewing lesson.

CHAPTER 9

"Deborah, here's something from Mark's Gospel that I decided to use," said my father. "You've mentioned before that too many of the stories about Jesus just look at him and other adults. But in this story you can see Jesus meeting and talking with some children and their mothers."

There wasn't much action in Mark's account. It was too short to figure out what was really going on. But I told my father that I would try writing a story with someone younger than me telling about what might have happened.

David's Story

(Luke 18:15-17)

I met Jesus when I was little. I don't think that I could have been more than five or six years old at the time. In the morning of the day we met him, I wasn't expecting anything unusual. I was hoping to stay in bed late and sleep. I love to sleep. But my mother had something else in mind.

"David," she called. I felt her shaking me. "Get up."

I pulled the blanket over my head. That makes her leave me alone sometimes. But not that day. As soon as the shaking stopped, I pretended to myself that I had only dreamed about her voice. She was probably outside talking to someone. I started telling myself that I must have dreamed that she had shaken me. I was almost asleep again when I heard a very real sound.

"David," her voice was real enough now. "If you don't get out of that bed, you'll wish you had."

I've learned to recognize that tone. Out I rolled. She uses that tone when she wants me to do something. I hoped it wasn't going to be hard.

"Put on your good clothes, David," she said. "Your sisters are already dressed. I'm taking all of you out today. You're going to get blessed."

This word "blessed" was a new one to me. I wasn't sure what it meant.

"Is it going to hurt?" I asked.

She looked at me like I was crazy. Then she laughed.

"Of course not, silly," she answered. "When you get blessed, some holy person puts his hands, or her hands, on you and then says a prayer that you will grow up to be happy."

I was still sleepy and wondering if there was some way for me to get out of going.

"What's the use of that, Mother?" I asked. "Couldn't they say their prayer without us going to them? Maybe it would be just as good for us to stay at home today. If they're really holy, shouldn't their prayers be able to work even when we aren't there? Why don't we just stay home?"

My mother didn't even look at me.

"I notice that you're not getting ready," she said even though she wasn't looking in my direction. That familiar tone was slipping into her voice again. I started getting ready

as she walked into the kitchen. "We aren't going to stay home today because I'm taking you and your sisters out. The three of you are going to get blessed by the prophet Jesus. If he blesses you, good things are going to happen."

There was no telling what good things she had in mind. But I had a good idea of what bad things might happen if I didn't get moving. We weren't going to stay home that day. There would be no more sleep for me until nap time.

Before I had my good clothes on, I rolled up my blanket and the little mat I sleep on. My mother was in the other room and I was alone in the room where we sleep. I wondered out loud about who this Jesus was. I had never heard of him.

After my bedding was put away, I changed into my good

clothes. I must have still been sleepy because Mother thought I was going too slow.

"Have you gone to sleep again?" she called from the kitchen. "I better not find you lying down."

"No, ma'am," said I, running into the kitchen to get something to eat.

She made me turn around so that she could see that I was dressed properly.

"Good job," she said. (She likes to make sure that I look all right.) "You're quite the little man. Here's breakfast."

Breakfast was leftovers from last night. At breakfast we usually eat the leftovers from the night before. That's because food spoils so quickly out here. It starts to smell bad and doesn't taste good unless you eat it in a day or so after it's fixed. Someone once told me that there are far away places where it is cool all the time and that you can keep food in your house for several days before it goes bad. That may be the way things are in the mountains or in big cities like Rome, but they're not that way here. We ate the leftovers from the night before. We also got some fresh goats' milk to drink.

When we finished eating, I was ready to go. I was standing at the door.

"Calm down, David," said my mother. "We have to wait for your aunt Rachel and my friend Leah from down the street. They're coming with their children too. Until they get here, you'll just have to be patient."

I sat down. Then I stood up and walked over to the window. No one was in sight. I sat down again. My mother was talking to my two baby sisters. Nothing important was being said. And, anyway, they can't understand what people say to them. I got up and walked over to the window. No one was in sight. We always have to wait for my mother's friends. I sat down. A few minutes later I got up and walked to the window.

"What do you think you're doing?" my mother asked me.

"I'm looking to see if they're here yet."

"You'll know when they get here. Just sit down, David. You're making me nervous."

I tried to sit still. I waited patiently. In a few minutes I was wondering if the morning had passed into afternoon. Would lunch be soon? Maybe I could take a nap.

Mother was still talking to my baby sisters. She was brushing their hair. Since they can't talk back, I never thought her talking to them made much sense. And she keeps telling them how pretty they are. I'm thinking that they are going to be spoiled. I could tell that I was getting bored. Since I had been sitting still for so long, I felt my foot going to sleep. I needed to move around.

"Mother," I said. She stopped brushing their hair. She looked at me in a way that meant I was interrupting her. "Who is this Jesus we're going to see?"

"Jesus?" she echoed. She started brushing the girls' hair again. "He's just some man."

She wasn't paying any attention to me. Ever since those two girls came around—they're twins, by the way—Mother has been wild about them. She holds them and sings to them and treats them special. Mother says she did the same thing for me when I was a baby, but I certainly don't remember it.

"Mother, you aren't listening to me."

She looked at me and stopped brushing their hair.

"I'm sorry, David. I wasn't paying attention. What did you want to know?"

"Who's Jesus?"

Mother started brushing their hair again. But at least she had heard my question this time. She was thinking of an answer.

"Jesus is a prophet," she explained. "He's a holy man who travels around the country telling people that God is going to set up his kingdom on the earth. There are stories that Jesus is able to make strange things happen. Sick people have become well. Blind people have learned to see. That sort of thing. He is a very wise man."

"Is he wise like the judges we saw at the Temple in Jerusalem when we went there for the holy days?"

"He's wiser than them, I expect. He's more like a teacher. You'll learn all about teachers once you start going to school. I've heard that Jesus teaches people how they ought to live."

Since Mother was paying attention to me, I decided to continue with the questions. I love it when she talks to me.

"And how is it that we are supposed to live?"

"God wants us all to be good. Being good is not just for boys and girls, but for grownups too."

"But I thought that grownups always were good."

My mother got a strange look in her face. She was starting to speak, but then there was a knock at the door.

"Come on in!" she shouted.

In came Aunt Rachel and her six children. Aunt Rachel is a few years older than my mother. But just because she's older doesn't mean that she's smarter. I can't understand why anyone would want to have six children. They make so much noise. The babies are always crying and slobbering, and the bigger kids are constantly getting into trouble.

I don't like to be around Aunt Rachel's kids when they're all together. But I have to admit that I do like her boy Jeremiah. He's my age, and we can do things together, that is, if the older kids don't bother us.

Jeremiah and I went outside to play as soon as Aunt Rachel and my mother started talking. We threw rocks against the wall of the house until Leah and her children came. Another one of our neighbors, Ada, was right behind her. Everyone was here now.

Our mothers called us inside. They made us dust off our clothes. They said that we had to look nice or else Jesus wouldn't like us. That sounded a little funny. I mean, since

this Jesus was supposed to be so wise, he ought to be able to meet kids without getting upset about how they were dressed. But it didn't seem like a good idea to mention that. And if Jesus were the kind of person who wouldn't like you if you had a little dust on your clothes, I didn't think I would like him. But it didn't seem like a good idea to mention that either.

After our mothers had inspected all the kids, off we marched. It was still early in the morning. Mother said it was hours until lunch. The weather wasn't hot, but because I had been playing with Jeremiah, I felt a little sweaty. I wanted to trot over to the well and have a drink of water. But Mother didn't look like she would approve. We kept on walking.

In a quarter of an hour we were outside the town and headed towards the hills where Jesus and his followers were camped. Within a few minutes we saw them standing around under the trees talking. I was too young to be able to count all the men there, but I could tell that several different things were going on. The men were divided into four groups.

There was one man by himself under a tree. At first I thought he was sleeping, but then I realized that it looked like he was praying. But he wasn't pulling his hair, or moaning, or waving his arms. A lot of people say you need to do those things so that God will listen to you. I don't think he was even moving his lips.

Off on our right side were two men talking about money. One of them was talking about how much money he used to make before he followed Jesus. It didn't sound as if he was sorry to have made the change though. The man with him was talking about how much money he was taking in now. ("That is, for the group of us, I mean," the second man said when the other one looked at him funny.) This second man had a large purse at his side.

There was another group between us and the prophet Jesus. (We all assumed that Jesus was the man praying.) There were four or five in this group. They were strong-looking, big men with muscles. They were talking about fishing. They were telling stories like any other fisherman you ever heard. As soon as one finished his story, another would chime in and explain how he had caught a bigger fish than the first one. You could see them spreading their hands to show how big their fish had been.

The last group was the largest. I couldn't count how many men were in it. They were talking about how tired they were. Several of these men were looking at one man's feet. He had a big blister on his heel. The others were discussing the best treatment for blisters.

No one seemed especially excited or in a hurry to do anything. We watched them for several minutes. I could tell that our mothers didn't know what we were supposed to do. We didn't want to bother Jesus.

"That one praying must be Jesus," said Aunt Rachel. "Surely he wouldn't mind a brief interruption. It looks like he's almost finished too."

"You're right," responded my mother. "Let's walk over to him."

But no one moved. We were still too shy to go. No one wanted to bother him while he was praying. After we stood there for a few minutes, I decided we couldn't stand there all day. If we were going to get blessed, and have the chance to get home for lunch and a nap, we might as well get on with it. I took a few steps towards Jesus. The rest of our group followed.

The men standing around noticed us coming. They stopped their talking and storytelling.

"Hey!" shouted one of the fishermen. "Where do you think you're going?"

"Please, sir," said Rachel. "We want the prophet to bless our children. Please let us see him."

"Can't you see that he's praying?" asked one of the men in the blister group. He looked tired and his feet must have been hurting. He was soaking his feet in a puddle of water.

"You'll have to come back later," said another man.

"Yes, come back later in the day," said the one with sore feet. "Until then, leave the master in peace."

I heard one of the men say to his group, "How can you expect him to pray when all these kids are around?" But I didn't see who was talking. It must be easier to serve God when you don't keep getting interrupted by people.

None of us wanted to go home. But the men with Jesus had told us to come back later. We stood there looking at the men. But they went back to their other activities. They ignored us.

Just then I noticed that Jesus had stopped praying. He was looking at us. He waved for us to come over. He smiled as we approached.

One of the men saw us going over. He started to say something, but Jesus didn't let him.

"Always let the little children come to me," said Jesus.

"You don't have to send them away. God's kingdom belongs to those who have hearts like these little ones."

Jesus then talked to us. He asked us our names and then remembered them well enough to call each of us by the right name. He told us a few stories. I wish I could remember what they were, but I was enjoying sitting there in the shade so much that I can't remember anything he said. I felt a little sleepy.

For a few minutes, I forgot about being thirsty or sweaty or worried about a big bully who lives down the street. I thought that my problems weren't important. I was glad to be there with my mother and sisters and cousins and friends. It was good.

None of us can remember how long we were there. It might have been an hour, but it could have been only a few minutes. After Jesus stopped speaking, he looked at us. We could tell it was time to go. He didn't say anything. But we knew he had other things to do.

"Thank you for being with us," said my mother.

Jesus smiled and said we were welcome any time. He said goodbye to each of us and remembered our names too when he said goodbye. He waved when we left. We waved back.

Our mothers talked about how they had had a good time. One of them, I think it was Leah, said that she had felt like a little girl again. Suddenly Aunt Rachel stopped all of us.

"Oh, darn," she said. "We forgot to have him bless the children."

CHAPTER 10

My father Luke heard the story about Zacchaeus from a traveler. It doesn't show up in Mark, and we never found it written down on any piece of papyrus or in any scroll. The man who told us the story was a Roman official traveling through Greece on government business. When he visited with our church, my father had asked him why he had become a Christian. The man said because another person who worked for the government had told him about Jesus. Our churches include all kinds of people, and what is interesting is that most of them who joined us when they were grown up did so because they heard other people talking about Jesus.

Nathan's Story

(Luke 19:1-10)

Nathan is what people are supposed to call me. Some kids call me "Shorty" when they first meet me. I don't mind that very much any more, but a few months ago anyone who called me "Shorty" found that their little bit of name-calling and making fun of me was followed by a quick (and hard) punch in the nose. Lots of boys think that a short person like me can't defend himself. They are mistaken. I have dished out far more black eyes and bloody noses than I have ever got here in the town of Jericho.

My father is Zacchaeus. He is a very important man in this area. I'll admit that he's on the short side too. And, just like me, he doesn't like it when people make fun of him. But he's never had to lift a finger to get even with anyone who bothered him. Father's rich. Because of his money and influence, he can cause trouble for people who laugh at him.

My father has made his money in business. He is a tax collector. Many years ago he had been appointed the chief tax collector for our area of Palestine. Now I've heard there are places where tax collectors get a salary. That is, they get paid a certain amount of money for the year no matter how much tax they collect.

But it doesn't work that way in the Roman Empire. Under the current system, the governor tells my father how much money he is supposed to turn over to the government's treasury at the end of the year. Once my father learned how much tax money was due, he took a troop of soldiers and then went throughout Jericho and the surrounding territory forcing people to pay up. And it was up to my father to decide how much money everyone had to pay him.

He always managed to collect more money than the governor demanded. But my father didn't have to return this extra money to the tax payers. He got to keep it for himself! By taking in more taxes than were required by the governor, my father became one of the richest men in Jericho.

Before our family met Jesus, my father used to tell me that he was in the best business in the world. He used to joke about it and say that his job was relieving people of their excess money. Furthermore, since he had Roman soldiers to back up his requests for tax money, sooner or later everyone paid what they were told to pay. There was nothing wrong in what he did, my father used to say. After all, everybody else who was a tax collector did the same thing.

Well, you can already guess that the citizens of Jericho weren't likely to give my father any popularity prizes. Some people said that he was a crook and worthless sinner. Others said that he was a traitor to the Jewish people since he cooperated with the Roman government.

Of course no one dared to say those things to his face. But, behind his back, people sometimes talked about how much they hated him. I remember hearing grownups in the marketplace telling one another stories about the wicked things he was supposed to have done. I guess these grownups didn't know who I was. They must have thought it was safe to gossip about my father in front of someone who was just a kid. But they learned a lesson about saying things about me and my family because, after I heard what they had to say, I made sure I found out their names so that I could tell my father what I had heard. He knew how to take care of people like them.

But he wasn't the only one who defended the family honor. I did my share too. I often fought with boys who made fun of us. Sometimes I'd hear a group of kids laughing about the way my father dressed or about my size. I wouldn't let people get away with that kind of thing. My usual plan was, after I picked up some rocks or a stick, I'd charge into the group and start swinging. My policy was to hit at anything that moved. Once one or two of the kids fell down, the rest would run away. I've been beaten up too, but I won more often than I lost.

My worst experience in a fight was right before we met Jesus. There were three boys hiding in an alley. I was walking

past and heard them mention my name. I stopped to listen.
They couldn't see me. After a few minutes they said that
I was too tough to mess with. I liked hearing that. But then
they started making fun of my father. I lost control of
myself.

Running into the alley, I found them standing together.
The biggest one got my fist in his face. POW! He fell to
the ground. But as I turned to the next biggest, the two standing grabbed me by the arms. They held me while the first
one beat me up. When they heard someone coming, they
ran away.

I was a sight. They had knocked out one of my teeth—
luckily it was a baby tooth—, blackened an eye, and given
me a bloody nose. I sat in the dust and cried until I could
walk back home.

My father was the first to see me. He was sitting in the
front room.

"Have you been fighting again, Nathan?"

"Yes, sir."

"Were the boys calling you 'Shorty'?"

"No." I didn't want to look at him.

"Why were you fighting then?"

My nose was hurting and I rubbed it with the back of my hand. It still hurt. I didn't want to answer him.

"Come on, son. Why were you fighting?"

I began crying again. I couldn't help it.

"There were some boys making fun of you," I said. "They said you were a cheap, little crook who ought to be spanked instead of respected. They called you a runt and a thief. I had to do something."

My father looked sad. "Go wash your face," he said. "Don't let your mother see you like that."

I had almost left the room when he called me back.

"Nathan, from now on you're not to fight with boys in the town. No matter what you hear them saying, I don't want you to fight. Even if it's about me. Do you understand?"

He was being serious. I nodded my head and left the room.

At dinner my mother didn't say anything about my black eye or missing tooth. She must have noticed them though. When I saw her looking at me, I felt like I needed to explain.

"Mother, there were these six boys," I started to lie. "They were calling me names. They said I was—"

"Don't go any further," said my father. "I've told her the whole story."

No one spoke during the rest of the meal. After dinner my parents sent me to bed without dessert. Since I don't normally go to bed that early, I couldn't go to sleep. I could hear them downstairs talking.

"Zacchaeus, I'm worried about our Nathan," said my mother. "Those horrible boys might really hurt him some day."

"I'm worried about that too. But it isn't likely he'll be doing more fighting. I've told him to stop. I think he'll obey me on this."

There was a pause. I could hear my father get up and start to pace. He was walking back and forth across the room.

"My real concern," said my father, "is what is happening to Nathan on the inside." Listening to my parents from my room, I started wondering about what my father meant. Could it mean that he thought that there was something wrong with me? I sure couldn't see how there was anything wrong with me. It's the other kids in our town who are the trouble-makers. I only finish what they start. And if a few people get hurt when things get settled up, that's their problem.

My father continued to talk.

"I wonder what kind of man he will become," he said. "I don't want him to grow up and be someone like me. I don't want him to spend his life looking for ways to get even with people."

My mother said something softly. I couldn't hear what it was.

"No, I don't think so," he said. "I wish I could start over, Martha. I don't like myself. I wish there was some way I could make a fresh start."

My mother said something again.

"Thanks," he said to her. "But I'm simply not happy. I'd like to be different. I wish I could be a new person. I just don't know how."

My parents stopped talking. The house was quiet.

I cried myself to sleep that night. (And it wasn't just because my nose was hurting.)

The next day my father came home excited. It wasn't that he was happy but that he was interested in something.

"Jesus the prophet is coming to Jericho," he explained.

"People say that he's able to make men and women change. He gives them a new chance at life. One of the tax collectors from the north told me about him. I would like to meet him!"

"Could you invite him over for dinner?" asked my mother.

"There's an idea," said my father with a cheerful note in his voice. Then he frowned. "Maybe not. What holy man is likely to eat with a tax collector? What holy man would eat with someone like me?"

We were quiet for a few moments.

"I'd still like to meet him though," said my father.

The day after that my father and I went out to meet Jesus. My mother was staying home to look after my smaller brother and older sister. While the two of us walked into the heart of town, my father spoke about starting life over. I couldn't figure out what he was talking about. But I guessed that Jesus would let him know something about it.

Things never work out the way you plan though. There were too many people for us to get through the crowd. By the time we got to the road where Jesus would be walking, people were standing five and six deep along the sides of the highway. We were too short to see over their heads. It appeared that we wouldn't get to see him after all. My father looked sad.

He seemed so hurt that I felt like I needed to do something. I noticed a large sycamore tree next to the road.

"Look over there, Father," I said and pointed. "I'll go climb that tree and tell you what he looks like."

I ran over to the tree, grabbed a branch, and started to pull myself up. There was a sudden noise at my side. It was my father. He was climbing the tree too!

I couldn't believe it. There was my father in his expensive clothes climbing a tree. He normally talks a lot about his dignity. He doesn't want to let people see him when he

isn't at his best. And there he was climbing the tree. He pulled himself into the branches as if he were a boy.

Some of the men in the crowd noticed us. They turned and pointed at us. A few were about to laugh when they recognized my father. They just turned away. But I could tell they thought the whole thing was funny. I must have looked funny too. (Remember that I still had my black eye and missing tooth.) But my father didn't seem to mind.

A little later Jesus came by.

The crowd hushed as people who recognized him poked one another, pointed at him, and whispered, "Yes, that's the prophet Jesus."

Everyone was hoping that Jesus would stop and teach a lesson from the Scriptures or tell a story or two. After all, Jericho is a famous town, and a lot of us were standing there, waiting for him to do something. Then Jesus stopped. One of his friends was speaking quietly to him. We all wondered what he was going to say.

One of Jesus' friends motioned with his hands for us to get quiet. The prophet Jesus was going to say something. Then, instead of beginning a talk about Moses or telling us one of his stories, Jesus looked up into the tree where we were sitting. He pointed.

"Zacchaeus," he shouted. "Come on down."

Everyone stared at us. I wondered if Jesus and the people were going to make fun of us. I was getting ready for trouble. For a second I wished that there were some Roman soldiers around. Then Jesus said something that I certainly didn't expect.

"Zacchaeus, I'll be staying in your house today."

My father grabbed a lower branch and then swung himself to the ground. He walked rapidly over to Jesus and the disciples. He smiled at Jesus. He smiled at the disciples. He even knew one of them, the one named Matthew. My father greeted them as honored guests. I couldn't remember seeing him look so happy for a long time.

But not everyone was happy about my father's meeting with Jesus. I could hear their whispering.

"Doesn't Jesus know what kind of man that Zacchaeus is?" asked Seth the baker. "That worthless tax collector is the biggest sinner in Jericho."

"You're right about that," whispered someone in reply. "If Jesus were really a holy man, he wouldn't even be seen with the likes of Zacchaeus."

"We've certainly learned something about Jesus," said Seth again. "You can bet he knows what side his bread is buttered on."

That got a laugh, but I didn't stay to take note of the names of the people laughing. Father, Jesus, and the others were walking away and almost out of sight. I started to follow them home but didn't want to get too close in case one of the holy people there told me to get lost. But then my father waved for me to come to him. I came closer.

"Run home and tell your mother that we're coming," he said.

I ran home. The hard thing was getting my mother to believe that company was going to be there in a few minutes. She likes to have lots of notice before people come to see us. She set me and the servants right to work on chores around the house.

There must have been a deep conversation between Jesus and my father as they walked to our house. Even when they came into our place they kept talking. They talked in private for what must have been a long time. I wasn't able to listen because I was too busy doing things for Mother. Still, there were a few things that I did hear.

One of the strangest things that they talked over was about how people change. I can remember my father talking about how he was unhappy being the man he was. He wanted a new start in life. He wished that he could be a different person. But Jesus didn't say the logical thing, that that sort of change was impossible. Instead Jesus said that it was sometimes necessary for men and women to start their lives over again. He said that we all need to figure out what kind of life we want to live and then we need to start living that way.

It was an odd conversation. But it must have made an impression on my father. He said that he was going to become a new person. As he got started talking, he even promised that he would divide up his wealth and give half to the poor.

"And if I've ever cheated anyone on their taxes," he went on, "I'll repay that person four times what I took."

Jesus must have understood that to be the proper ending to their conversation.

"Today," said Jesus to the people gathered in the living room, "salvation has come to this house."

I wasn't sure about the meaning of the word "salvation," but I never like to let people know that there are things I don't understand. Anyway, there was no one around that I could ask about it.

Then Jesus pointed at my father. "Truly this man is a son of Abraham."

That was a great compliment. All Jews like to be compared with our father Abraham, who lived almost two thousand years ago and who first served God in Israel. But I wasn't able to listen further. It was back to work with my mother.

The group of us ate dinner together. Jesus and his disciples were polite during the meal. Although everyone had the chance to say something, Jesus did most of the talking.

When the group of disciples and Jesus left, my parents spoke together for some time. They didn't send me away. I asked my parents about this "salvation" stuff.

"It's like a parable Jesus told about a woman losing some money," said my father. "When she realized it was gone, she looked everywhere in her house until she found it. The money was useless until it was found. That's the way I felt, Nathan. I felt that I was useless, but now things are going to be different."

Since the day Jesus came into our home, my parents have been changing. They don't talk about money as much as they used to. They're not as concerned about impressing other rich people in the city. My father is giving away lots of his money to the poor. My mother has sold most of her jewelry.

At first the citizens of Jericho thought that my parents had gone crazy. They couldn't understand what was happening to them. But now some of those who used to despise my father are beginning to realize that he is a different person. Of course, there are many who still hate him, but more and more people are admitting that he does seem to be a new man.

My parents are even starting to make new friends. They're meeting people who like them for who they are and not for what they have. I remember how my father once said that the only "friends" he had were those people who needed favors. But things are changing here too.

My father had another talk with me about fighting. He explained that it just wasn't worth the trouble.

"What's the point of it?" he asked. "If what kids say is true, why bother? You can't make yourself taller by hitting someone in the face. You might feel better for a few minutes after you hit another person. But eventually you'll be knocked down, beaten up, and still be somewhat on the short side."

That made some sense.

"And if what other kids are saying isn't true," he went on, "what's there to get upset about? Just because a person doesn't have enough brains to tell the difference between what's true and what isn't true is no reason for you to try to beat some sense into those brains. Why waste your time on someone who's that ignorant?"

From the time my parents and I met Jesus, I haven't been in a single fight. I've come close. I've raised my fists, but thinking back to what my father said has made a difference. I've even walked away from trouble and have, more than once, pretended that I didn't hear what I really heard someone say.

Right now I'm even starting to make some friends. That's a new experience for me. And, even though it's a new experience, it does seem that being friendly with other kids is more fun than fighting. In fact, I'm starting to get to know some of the boys I've fought with. A few of them might even turn out to be all right.

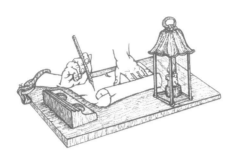

CHAPTER 11

One afternoon I could tell that my father was puzzled about something. He had been reading and writing by himself at the church that day while I had been doing things around the house. There was a packet of letters being passed from church to church in Greece that had come to our own church the day before. The letters were copies of the letters of advice which had been written by famous Christians in the past. But along with the letters, he found a short account of what had happened to Mary the mother of Jesus before Jesus had been born.

That story about Mary had him puzzled. I asked him what was wrong with it.

"Nothing is really wrong," he said. "It's just that there are so many different stories about how Jesus was born. In most of the stories I've seen, people talk as if Jesus was born like any other child. But the story I just finished reading says just the opposite. It says that God was Jesus' Father."

"But God is everyone's Father."

"It's true that we all come from God, Deborah. But the story I just read agrees with the Christians who say that Jesus didn't have a human father at all. It says that the Spirit of God came to Mary and she became pregnant in a super-natural way."

"Well, if you believe this account, you'll just have to change what you've written so far in your gospel."

He thought for a few minutes.

"I don't know if I want to do that. In the other parts of my gospel I talk about Joseph being the father of Jesus. That is, everyone seems to call Jesus the son of Joseph. Nothing in Mark's Gospel or the Letters of Paul suggest that Jesus was born in anything except the normal way. I even found a genealogy of Joseph, which traces back Jesus' ancestors from Joseph to Adam and then to God. There wouldn't be any point in giving that family history unless Joseph was Jesus' father. The first followers of the Lord wouldn't have bothered to remember Joseph's ancestors unless they thought Joseph was the real father of Jesus."

"Then leave the new story about the Holy Spirit and Mary out. Don't change anything in your gospel."

"I don't want to do that either. It's a good story. It says a lot about how God works in our world. And Mary gives a beautiful prayer in the story. I would like to use it in my gospel."

He was quiet again. He started to rub the side of his head. (He does that when he's trying to make up his mind about something.)

"What do you intend to do, Father?"

"I guess the best thing to do is to write down everything I have. I'll leave in the conversations and descriptions where Jesus is called the son of Joseph, and I'll leave in the genealogy of Joseph. But I'll also include the story of Mary being the virgin mother of Jesus. Even though some other Christian writers don't mention this, it's certainly not up to me to say that it is impossible that Mary gave birth to Jesus when she was still a virgin. I believe God could do that."

132

He paused for a moment and then went on. "Who can say what will happen? In the future it may even happen that some of the Christians who read our gospels will say that it really doesn't matter that much anyhow. In any case, no matter how Jesus was conceived and born, his birth has to count as a miracle."

I nodded my head. Before he could start rubbing the side of his head again, I interrupted his thoughts.

"When can I read what you've written, Father?"

"As soon as I'm finished, but I haven't written the full account of Jesus' birth yet," he said. "Wait a minute though. I've got part of it done now. There's a section you'll probably like. In fact, I think you might want to use the last part of the account when you write your own story."

Jesse's Story

(Luke 2:1-20)

My father is a shepherd. His name is Samuel. My own name is Jesse.

Last winter my father decided that I was old enough to start helping him take care of our family's sheep. He was at home then, spending a few nights with us in the village. I remember him telling my mother what he had decided. He thought that I was ready to go out into the hills with him and the sheep. He also said that he was needing the help because our flock was growing and there were lots of lambs to look after. He wanted me to go with him and the other shepherds into the hills that surround our town of Bethlehem.

As good Jews we are proud to live in Bethlehem. The great King David, who had also been a shepherd, was born in Bethlehem over one thousand years ago. In these many years since the time King David lived, some of our prophets have said that another king would come from our city.

The prophets said that this king was going to save God's chosen people, us Jews, from some kind of trouble. But they never explained what kind of trouble he would rescue us from. And they never told us exactly when he was coming.

But back to my story. My mother was worried about me leaving home. Even though my father said he needed help looking after the sheep, Mother thought that I was still too young. She knows that the life of a shepherd is not as easy as many people think.

My friend John, who has lived all his life in the city, thinks that shepherds are lazy. He says that they spend their days lying around and watching the clouds. Looking after sheep isn't at all exciting, as far as he is concerned. He says that bakers, like his father and big brothers, have more important jobs.

I admit that I don't know a thing about being a baker. But I do know that shepherds work harder than most people realize. They have to make sure that the sheep get enough grass to eat and enough water to stay healthy. We also have to watch out for robbers. And there are times, when we shepherds are out in the hills, that we have to guard the sheep from all kinds of wild animals. Sometimes a bear or lions will try to eat the sheep.

My mother didn't like the idea of me protecting our sheep from lions or bears. That was the first reason she gave for not wanting me to go. She also said that I wasn't old enough. But my father said that he had been my age when he first started looking after sheep. They talked about this for a long time. They kept talking, even after the sun went down. Even in the dark house, long past the time we usually go to sleep, they talked. I don't know how long they were awake. After I woke up the next morning though, my mother told me that she agreed that I could go with my father.

Two days later my father and I said goodbye to my big sisters. They were staying at home in Bethlehem. My father and I were off to the hills.

We walked away from the city and farms. Once we got into the hills, we started searching for my uncle. Uncle Noah is my father's brother. He too is a shepherd and also has his house in Bethlehem. He and my father often look after one another's sheep when one of them wants to go back home for a visit.

We found Uncle Noah sitting beside a tall tree with his face to the sun. He was watching the sheep munching their way through the grass. When we were close enough for him to hear us, we yelled in his direction. He saw us and waved.

"Hello, Jesse," he said to me when we were all sitting together, enjoying the heat from the sun. "So you're finally going to become a shepherd like the rest of us. It's good to have you here."

Then Uncle Noah began a report to my father.

"Nothing much has happened while you were away," he said. "No one has heard of any robbers. There's been no signs of wild animals. The sheep are fine and fat. Just look at them."

We looked at them.

"Really the only thing I have to complain about," he went on, "is how cold it's getting at nights. Up until now the weather has been mild, but these last few nights have been cold. The sheep huddle together to stay warm when they sleep. By the way, did you remember to bring an extra blanket for me?"

We said yes.

"Still the nights haven't been totally miserable," he said. "There's been that big, bright star to give me company. It really cheers me up."

We gave Uncle Noah the blanket he wanted. Father pointed to the clouds in the west and asked if they looked

like snow clouds. Uncle Noah said maybe yes and maybe no. I told Uncle Noah that we had been watching the big, bright star too. I had first seen it when we were back in Bethlehem.

Just in case you don't know what star I'm talking about, I will tell you something about it. People had first noticed it a few weeks ago. There were some who said that it was an old, familiar star which suddenly got brighter. Others said it was totally new. There were even a few people who said that it wasn't a single star at all. They said it was really two or three stars, or perhaps planets, that had moved closer together so that it looked like one big star.

I certainly don't know who was right. I'm a shepherd, not an astronomer. I've never paid much attention to the stars. But my parents have told me many of the stars' names and some of their stories, but I can't seem to remember them. Still there's no doubt that the new star was bright and brilliant. It had a twinkle and a sparkle that made you almost think that it was alive. Who knows? Maybe it was alive. Some people say that the stars are alive and that they too are creatures made by God.

Of course there were grouches in Bethlehem who said that anything out of the ordinary like this star means that something bad is going to happen. These are the same people who think that anything new or different means trouble. But probably most people in Bethlehem ignored the star. They said that they had enough to do without worrying about the stars.

But my father said there was something special about the star. He said that it was a sign, a sort of reminder, sent from God to us.

"What's it supposed to remind us of?" I asked.

"Of everything important," he said in a quiet voice.

That, of course, was no answer, but I could tell by the way he looked that he was pleased with himself for that answer.

Now that I've said something about the star, I'll get back to my story again. Uncle Noah, my father, and I sat in the sun with our backs next to the tree. We watched the sheep. If one of them started to wander away from the rest, my father would send me over to bring it back.

After I carried back a lamb which kept trying to lose itself, I found that my father and uncle were talking about the troubles in Bethlehem. The city was very crowded. It seems that Caesar Augustus, the Roman Emperor, wanted to know how many people were in the Empire. (Why knowing this was important was never explained to me.) Anyway, Caesar ordered a thing called a 'census.' A 'census' is when the people of a country get counted by the government. To make this counting easier for the Roman officials, everyone was supposed to go into one of the bigger towns or cities here in Palestine.

"I know that seems like a dumb way to count," said my father. "But that's the government for you."

Bethlehem is a city where many families have come from. Even during normal times it is full of people. But since the census was being held, the city was absolutely packed. There were hundreds and hundreds of extra people in town. They were the sons and daughters and grandchildren of parents and grandparents who had once lived in Bethlehem.

Since our family had always lived in Bethlehem, we didn't have to do any traveling in order to be counted. But many folks weren't so lucky. Thousands of children, parents, and old people all over Palestine had to walk to get to the places where they were supposed to be counted.

All of the hotels and houses in Bethlehem were filled. But, even in spite of that, more people kept coming into the city. Everyone we knew in town already had a house full of relatives. Neither my father nor uncle could imagine where there was supposed to be room for all of the folks who came to be counted.

To give an example of how bad things were getting, my father told about how many travelers were being forced to sleep and live in barns. Not only did these people have to stay in the barns with the smelly farm animals, but they also had to pay good money for the privilege of sleeping there.

After a lot more grownup talk about the crowded city and high prices, my father and uncle became silent. We sat and watched the sheep. In the late afternoon we led the sheep back into the fold (you might call this a 'corral'). That's where they spend the night protected by the fence. We counted the sheep as they went into the gate. We need to know where all the sheep are in the evening because a sheep that spends a night on its own outside the fold doesn't always make it back to the flock. But they were all there.

Once the sheep were inside the fence, we ate. Dinner was milk and cheese. A little later we said our prayers and went to sleep.

It was another cold night. I was glad the bright star shined over us. I missed my mother and my sisters and was feeling lonely. My father and uncle were asleep. I could hear their soft breathing. There was no one to talk to. At least the star was there to keep me company. It cheered me up. A little, anyway.

The next day was quiet and peaceful. Nothing out of the ordinary happened. We led the sheep out of the fold in the morning and walked with them over to the spot where they would spend the day. All day long we'd watch them chew grass. In the evening we'd take them back to the corral and sleep in the cold.

This sort of thing went on for several days. We would count the sheep morning and night, and spend our days with them. I was beginning to wonder whether my friend John had been right when he said that shepherds led very easy, but unexciting lives. By dinner of the fourth day, I was thinking that shepherds never did anything interesting.

But a little later, right before we were going to say our evening prayers, just after we had spread our blankets on the ground, another shepherd ran into our camp. I could see blood on his clothes. He was angry and shouting. He told us that a bear had attacked his flock. The bear had killed one sheep and carried it off. Two other sheep had been clawed. The shepherd said we would have to do something about the bear. We agreed. There was going to be a meeting the next day. We promised to go.

When the shepherd left, my father and Uncle Noah talked about bears. They told me to go to sleep and tried to speak softly so that I couldn't hear them. I suppose they didn't want to frighten me. Although I was a little nervous, in a few minutes I fell asleep.

But in the middle of the night I had a nightmare. I woke up with a little jump and might even have said something out loud. When I looked around the camp, I noticed that my father was awake. He was sitting next to our small fire and warming his hands. I think he had been humming to himself.

"Did you hear something, Jesse?" he asked when he saw me sitting up.

"I'm not sure. Did you?"

He laughed. I didn't want him to know that I had just had a nightmare and was still a little afraid to go back to sleep, but my question must have sounded funny.

For a few minutes we sat there looking at the star. Neither of us talked. Watching it twinkle made me calm down. When I was relaxed again, I asked him about what was on my mind.

"What are the shepherds going to do about the bear?"

"I don't know, Jesse. But there's no reason for you to be afraid of bears or anything else. As long as Noah and I are here looking after you, you're as safe as you would be in Bethlehem. We've handled bears before. Go back to sleep. We'll have a busy day tomorrow."

The sun was shining in a clear, cool sky when I woke up. My father and uncle were already awake eating breakfast. They must have let me sleep in, but they made me rush once I was awake. "Hurry up," they kept saying. Once we had the sheep safely in their pasture, we hurried to the shepherds' meeting. At last things were going to get exciting.

There was a lot of talk at the meeting. While the shepherds agreed that we needed to do something, we couldn't agree on exactly what needed to be done. Shepherd after shepherd gave his opinion on how to handle bears. Someone said to dig a pit. Someone else said we needed spears. Another person said we ought to throw rocks when the bear came. It took hours.

In the mid-afternoon we came up with our final plan. The shepherds would bring all the sheep together that night. We would be guarding the flocks and waiting. There were to be lookouts in the hills. If the bear came, we would be ready for him.

Only a few men really wanted to kill the bear. After all, the bear was hungry and, just like any other animal, a bear has to eat. But bears were supposed to eat other wild animals. We couldn't let him go on eating our sheep.

In the afternoon we went back to our sheep. I found the few who had wandered away. Then my father, Uncle Noah, and I gathered rocks and sticks. We would need them in case we had to fight the bear.

When we thought we had enough rocks, we led our sheep to the place where the other shepherds had gathered. As the sun went down, we ate dinner. Because there were so many of us, we turned the meal into a feast. We shared bread, fruit, and sweets with one another. There was plenty of milk and cheese. As we sat around the fires, the sheep huddled together in the cool night air.

Our lookouts went to their positions. Our fires went out. After it was dark, I could feel the cold numbing my hands and feet. I wrapped myself in a blanket and looked up at the star. It shone brighter than ever.

I was in the middle of a dream when there was a loud noise. Someone was shouting. Shepherds grabbed rocks and sticks. My father grabbed his staff. I picked up a handful of rocks. We were ready for the bear.

I could see something moving on the road. It was in the shadow, near the bottom of the hills. We circled around

the dark shape. Certainly it was big enough to be a bear.
Inside my chest my heart was beating hard. I got ready to
throw my first rock. But the shape we thought was a bear
stopped. It raised its arms.

"Hello," it said.

What we thought was a bear wasn't a bear at all. I was
glad I hadn't thrown my rock. The man stepped out from
the shadows. His clothes were light in color, perhaps even
white. When he was away from the shadows, the light of
the star shined on him and made his clothes seem to glow.
He looked important.

"Don't be afraid," he said as he walked toward us.

None of the shepherds said anything.

"I bring you, and all people everywhere, great news,"
he said. "This very night, in the city of David, a savior is
born for you. He is the Messiah, the Lord."

There was nothing for us to say.

"And this," he continued, "is how you will recognize him.

You will find the baby wrapped in a blanket and lying in a manger."

This was a very odd thing for a stranger on the road to say to a group of shepherds who were about to throw rocks at him. All this talk about the Messiah was confusing, especially since a manger is a box which holds animal food and didn't seem to be a good place for a baby to sleep. We didn't know what to say. All at once I noticed that the stranger had been joined by several other people. (Where did they come from?) They were dressed in the same kind of clothing. Their clothes almost glowed in the dark. I now could understand why the stranger had told us not to be afraid. If they had suddenly appeared all at once, I would have been scared.

Then the strangers started to sing.

"Glory to God in heaven," they sang. "And peace on earth to those of good will."

Their voices were wonderful. I was waiting for more singing when they disappeared. Surely what we had seen weren't people at all. They must have been angels. The silent night felt empty without them.

"Let's go down into Bethlehem and see this thing that the angels have told us about," said someone.

"But where shall we go?" asked my uncle. "Bethlehem is full of people."

"I have an idea," said my father. "Jesse and I were there just last week. I've even seen some of the barns that travelers were sleeping in."

So off we went to Bethlehem. Most of us were curious. We wanted to see what was going on. But there were a few shepherds who weren't excited about going into the town. They walked with us into Bethlehem, but they were slouching rather than walking straight. (Could it really be that there are people who don't want to know what things God is doing?)

When we reached Bethlehem, we searched for the barn. We went to the barns my father knew were being rented. Outside of one we could hear a baby crying. For a few minutes we stood outside the stable door wondering whether it was all right for us to enter. One of the shepherds knocked. I had never seen anyone knock on a barn door, but we didn't think it was proper to barge in without asking. A voice called out and said to come in.

In we went. There was a baby with his father and mother. The baby had stopped crying. His mother was feeding him and holding him at her side. But I could see that the baby had been lying in the manger. A manger is a very strange place to put a baby. There were animals in the barn too. Maybe they wondered what a baby was doing in their manger.

The mother was a young woman who couldn't have been more than twenty. She might have been fifteen or sixteen. She looked tired, but you could tell that she was happy. Her husband was older. You could tell by his arms and shoulders that he was a working man.

We told them why we had come. We wanted to see if what the angels said had been true. It was, at least according to everything we could see at the time. My father told how the angels had said that the baby would grow up to be someone important. The woman smiled.

My father left to get the rest of our family. He wanted them to see this baby too. Other shepherds left to bring their own families. People from the town stopped by. It was nice.

Someone noticed that the baby's family looked poorer than what you would expect for the parents of someone who was going to be important. A few people from the town gave them some food or money. It seemed like the least we could do. Everyone was unusually friendly. It was strange.

After a couple of hours my father said it was time for us to get back to our jobs and responsibilities. But I didn't mind going. The baby was asleep in his mother's arms. His mother was asleep too. It was time for us to go. Bakers left for their bakeries, mothers left for their families, farmers left for their fields, and we shepherds returned to our flocks.

The time was still before dawn. The sheep lay sleeping. Even though it was still dark, no one felt like sleeping. We sat together looking at the stars. When the sun came up, we led our sheep back to their pastures. After being awake all night, I slept most of the day.

I wish I knew what was going to happen to the baby. What will he be like when he grows up? The angels said he was going to be someone important. Will he be a teacher, a rabbi, a prophet? Perhaps he will be a general or a king and make our people free.

Oh, yes, to get back to my story, in case you are wondering about the bear we planned to trap. No one ever saw him again.

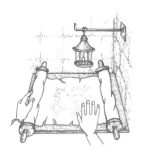

CHAPTER 12

"Deborah, here's something that I really don't know what to do with," said my father one morning.

He handed me a sheet of papyrus that was rolled up and held together by a cloth ribbon. The paper was still new. It wasn't discolored along any of the visible edges. When I unrolled the scroll, I saw that the inked letters were crisp and black. It looked as if it might have been written yesterday. I started reading it.

"It's a story about Jesus in Jerusalem," I said after reading the first few sentences. "I've never heard it before."

"I hadn't either."

When I finished reading, I rolled the sheet of papyrus and wrapped the ribbon around it. My father took it from my hands.

"It's a dramatic story," I said.

Father nodded. His hand moved towards the side of his forehead. There was still something on his mind.

"It's dramatic, all right," he said. "But I can't decide whether I want to use it or not."

"Why not?"

146

"For one thing I'm suspicious about the story."

"You mean that you don't think it could have happened?"

"Not exactly. It could have happened, all right. And if Jesus had ever been in a situation like that, I think he would have acted just the way the story goes. But it's so good that I think I would have heard of it before. And I'm also suspicious for another reason. The man who let me borrow this scroll said that the Apostle John had written this very report. He said that John had done it right after the incident."

"So?"

"Did you notice anything about the paper when you held it? You must have noticed that the papyrus was too fresh and that the ink was too black to be sixty years old."

"I noticed that. But doesn't that just mean that the Apostle John wrote the story and that someone else made a more recent copy?"

"That could be. But that's not what the man said to me. He stressed the fact that the Apostle John had written it on this very scroll."

"Oh." It was hard to think of why someone would say something like that if it wasn't true. "Well, what do you think happened then?"

"Someone, but we don't know who, might have made up this story to show how Jesus forgave people who were sinners. And then, because the writer wasn't sure that anybody would listen to the story unless it seemed to be written by somebody famous, like the Apostle John, he also went on to say that the Apostle John actually did write it. A lot of people do that sort of thing nowadays. Writers who aren't famous often have to write stories or letters and pretend that some famous person was the real author. I've seen it done lots of times."

"So that's why you won't use the story?"

"That's part of it. The other part is that in my gospel I already talk about how Jesus forgave sinners. And I think the stories I've used are based on things that really happened, even if there might be a little exaggeration in them. So, if you want my opinion, I won't use this story in my gospel, but if someone else writes another gospel in the future, it would be fine for him to use it if he wants to. It's still a great story. And the important thing, anyway, about stories in the gospels is whether or not they are true in showing what Jesus is like. The less important thing is being concerned about getting every single detail explained in its exact order. Overall it's the message that matters."

"So you're sure that you aren't going to use this story?"

"Yes. But if you want to in your own gospel, go ahead."

"I think I might then. I like this story even if it didn't happen."

Tabitha's Story

(John 7:53–8:11)

My mother calls me "Tabby" even though my real name is Tabitha. My mother is my best friend. I don't have a father.

Wait a minute though, that's not exactly right. I do have a father. It's just that I can't remember ever seeing him. He left my mother and me a few months after I was born. My mother hardly ever mentions his name. (I can't even remember it.) I don't know anything about him.

My mother is my best friend. In fact, she is the only friend I have. Back when I was younger, I tried to make friends with the other children in the neighborhood. But as soon as I started to get to know them, their mothers and fathers would find out about me. And, then, once they learned my name, they told their kids not to have anything to do with me. They said that I was a bad girl.

From then on, the kids around here have been mean to me. They used to tease me and laugh at me. It wasn't the nice kind of teasing that friends sometimes do with one another. It was a mean and spiteful thing they did to make me feel bad. They used to make fun of me until I cried. Then they would laugh all the more because I cried.

When I would ask them why they were so mean, they just laughed. They said that bad girls were supposed to feel bad.

I never knew why they said that. I had never hurt any of them. I only wanted to be friends. That didn't matter though. They said that I was a bad girl because my mother was bad.

And that didn't make any sense either. My mother has always been good to me. In fact, she is the only person who has ever been nice to me. She talks to me, plays with me, and takes me out with her when she goes to the marketplace. How can they call her bad?

One day I came home after some older boys had thrown rocks at me. I was crying. One of the rocks had cut my chin.

It was still bleeding when I met my mother. She wanted to know what happened. As soon as I stopped crying, I started to tell her.

"They said that bad girls like me were supposed to stay away from them. They said that I was 'unclean.' But I wasn't bothering them. I didn't even know that they were around. I was just out walking by myself. They just started throwing rocks at me for no reason."

I started crying again.

"Why do they do it, Mother? Why do they hate me?"

My mother looked sad.

"It's not your fault, Tabby. They don't like you because their parents don't like me. They all say that I'm no good. And, you might as well know it, they're right. Whether you believe it or not, they're right. I am no good."

"That's not true. You're a wonderful mother. You've always been good to me."

At that she started crying too. She held me in her arms and tried to keep talking. But we both kept crying while she talked to me.

"No, Tabby," she said and sniffed. "That doesn't matter. I am no good. I've done a lot of terrible things in my life. But there's been nothing else that I could do. No one cares about us. No one loves us."

I could feel her shaking.

"But, Mother, what about your friends?" I asked, hoping that she would stop crying. "Don't they care about you?"

"My what?" she asked.

She looked at me as if she hadn't heard me. Then she understood what I meant. She stopped crying and made some sounds that almost seemed to be laughing. But it wasn't a happy-sounding laugh. It was a laugh that sounded hard, the kind of laugh a person might have if he heard about someone he didn't like getting hurt. I didn't like to hear my mother make that kind of sound.

"Oh, *them*," she said. "Those men who come to see me aren't our friends. They don't care about us."

We sat there together for a long time. I cried, and she cried, but hugging one another made it feel less terrible. After a little while, one of my mother's men friends came over to see her. She wiped her face, put on some makeup, and told me to go outside. I stayed near the house so that those mean boys couldn't throw rocks at me again.

Pretty soon a whole bunch of men walked up to our house. Some of them were friends of my mother. But there were several other men that I had never seen before. They were wearing religious clothes so I knew that they had to be men of God. I wondered why they were all coming in a group to see my mother. We never go to synagogue, and we never bother the holy people we see.

I watched the men to see what they would do.

They wanted to break into the house! Instead of being polite and knocking, two of them kicked open the door and rushed in. Except for a couple who stood and watched the windows, the rest followed quickly inside. In about thirty seconds the man seeing my mother ran out of the house. He was in a hurry.

"Don't worry, Amos," said a man guarding one of the windows. "We'll keep your name out of this."

Then my mother was dragged outside the house. She didn't have all her clothes on and was just wrapped in one of our blankets. She was crying again.

I ran over to see what was wrong. But before I got to her, one of the leaders in the group pointed at me. He told the man who had kicked the door open to keep me out of the way.

"Mother, Mother!" I shouted as I ran toward her.

But the next thing I knew, there was a big hand over my mouth and I was being picked up. It was the man who was supposed to keep me out of the way. He picked me up

like a sack and put me under his arm. I tried to bite him, but I couldn't get my mouth open wide enough to chomp down on anything. I could barely breathe.

A couple of men started pushing my mother. They wanted her to walk with them. There was nothing I could do.

The group of us then started up the mountain in the center of town. We were going to the Temple. I had never been to the Temple before, but I was too busy to look at the buildings.

We walked up to a man who was teaching a class. On every day of the year there are teachers leading classes in the area right around the Temple. I've heard that many grownups go to the Temple just to listen in on the different teachers giving their lessons. The teacher we stopped by was reading from something. He put it down when the group of us came up. He didn't say anything to us.

Two of the leaders of our group pushed my mother at the teacher. She fell down into the dirt at his feet. No one had even said a word. Everything was quiet.

I knew I needed to get away to help my mother. I twisted around suddenly and had my mouth free. The only part that I could see on the man who was holding me was his hand. I bit it.

"Let me go," I squealed when he yanked his hand away.

But he only shifted his grasp, told me to shut up, and covered my mouth again.

One of the leaders from our group must have been a lawyer. He sounded like one. He was telling the teacher something. I hadn't heard the first part of what he said because that was when I was busy biting my guard's hand. But I did hear the last words he was saying.

". . . and, as you know perfectly well, in the Law of Moses it says that her kind deserves to be killed by stoning. What do *you* say?"

I couldn't believe my ears. "Stoning" is a punishment for criminals. The criminal is put into a pit and then people throw big rocks on him until he dies. This was what they wanted to do to my mother.

There was a change in the teacher's face. When we first arrived, he had been calm. The class looked as if they had been enjoying the lesson. But as soon as the lawyer asked his final question, the teacher became angry. He didn't say anything yet, but you could tell he was upset by his face.

Then, acting (I suppose) the way some people do when they count to ten before they say anything if they're mad, the teacher leaned over towards the dirt in the street. He started to draw, or maybe write, something in the dirt.

I couldn't really see what he was doing. (Sorry.) When I had tried to twist around to get a better look, my guard had squeezed me tighter. He had said that he had had about enough trouble from me.

"All right," said the teacher in a voice which sounded quite calm. I could see him moving his face so that he was making eye contact with all the men in our group, even my guard. "Go ahead and stone her, but let the one of you who is without sin throw the first rocks."

I couldn't believe my ears. I tried to shout no, but I couldn't open my mouth. The teacher had said it was all right for them to kill my mother. The teacher then bent over again and continued drawing (or writing) in the dirt.

But something strange was happening. An old man wearing a judge's robes turned his back on the rest of us and just walked away. My guard eased up on his hold on me. Two of my mother's friends glanced at one another. They made eye contact but didn't say anything. They walked away too. A priest, still wearing his religious clothes, rubbed his eyes. He walked back to the main entrance of the Temple. In a couple of minutes there was no one left from our group. Even the man holding me left. He had put me down about in the middle of all this.

"Sorry, kid," he said when he turned his back on me. He never looked at me.

The teacher and the class were still in the same spot. I myself couldn't move. My legs and arms were still shaking from struggling to break free. I wanted to go to my mother but couldn't control my body.

My mother looked horrible. She was wrapped in what

was now a very dirty blanket. Dust and dirt were on her face and in her hair. She was still crying. The lines made by her tears criss-crossed her face. She had rubbed her eyes and her makeup was smeared.

The teacher had stopped drawing (or writing) on the ground. He straightened himself up and walked to her. After trying to make eye contact with everyone left, he spoke to her.

"Woman, where are they now? Isn't there anyone left who wants to condemn you?"

My mother glanced around the area. Then she looked at him.

"None of them are left," she said.

"Very well, then," he said. "I won't condemn you either. Go back home, but sin no more."

Some of the women who were in the teacher's class helped my mother get wrapped up. They got her covered and walked home with us.

Since that day a few weeks ago things have changed. My mother's old friends don't come around anymore. She is getting a new set of friends. And, this time, some of her friends are women.

A few people from the class Jesus was teaching have started coming over to see us. (The teacher's name was Jesus.) A couple of the women have stopped by every day to see my mother.

Also coming by was a man, a lawyer, she used to know. He had been in the class that Jesus was teaching and recognized her that day. He looked familiar to me. I asked my mother if I was right in thinking that I had seen him before. She said that I might have but that that had been a long time ago. She told me not to mention it when anyone else was around.

The man is a lawyer here in the city. When he comes to see my mother, he always comes with two older women.

He explained to us that, since no one has seen my father in many years, they're checking to find out if he's dead. If they can find a witness to my father's death, my mother can be declared a widow. Right now, even though my father left us years ago, my mother is still considered legally married. She can't do certain legal things on her own until her legal status about being married gets cleared up. I don't understand all this legal stuff, but it seems to be important. All I know is that it's complicated.

After this law case is decided, we will move away from Jerusalem. Some of the followers of Jesus are teaching my mother a skill, weaving, so that she can have a job of her own. We may move in with a group of them in another city.

One day, a couple of weeks after the incident at the Temple, I asked my mother about what had happened. She hadn't mentioned it. I could tell that she didn't like to think about it. But on this day she seemed more relaxed. The law case she had started was almost over. The lawyer had finally found a witness who said that my father was dead. We were expecting to go before a judge any day now. My mother was happy that it would soon be over. That's what she said. Because of her good mood, I asked her about what had happened that day in the Temple.

"What did you do that was so wrong, Mother?" I asked. "Why did those men want to kill you?"

"First of all," she said, "you need to understand that those men didn't care about what I was doing. They weren't really interested in me at all. They just wanted to cause trouble for Jesus. I was being used by them to embarrass him."

She was quiet for a few moments. There was something else she wanted (but also didn't want) to tell me.

"But I had been doing something wrong, Tabby," she said. "It's hard to explain to you exactly what it was right now. But in a few years you'll understand better. This may help you understand though. You know that it is wrong to lie?"

"Of course."

"Well, there's a special way married people say 'I love you' to one another. A husband is only supposed to say that to his wife, and a wife is only supposed to say that to her husband. I was doing something wrong by saying 'I love you' to a lot of different men. I was lying to them."

"But doesn't that mean they were also lying to you?"

"Yes. We were telling lies to one another. But I don't think that any of us were fooled though. I know I wasn't."

Her face lost all expression as she stared at the floor. She wouldn't look at me.

"Mother," I said and touched her hand.

She looked at me.

"But things are different now, aren't they?" I asked.

"Yes, I think that they are."

"Mother, promise me that you'll never say that awful thing again."

"What did I say?"

"You know. On that terrible day you were saying that you were no good. You won't ever say that again, will you?"

"No, Tabby. I won't. I promise."

"Deborah," called my father Luke when he had finished reading this story. "This is good."

"Thanks." I felt shy and felt like I needed to say something else. "When you can start off with something that's already dramatic, it isn't that hard to write a good story."

"You did a fine job." He smiled and gave me a hug.

"Father, does it make you change your mind about the scroll, and the writing, and the Apostle John? Will you now want to use the story in your gospel?"

He just shook his head.

CHAPTER 13

It was months ago that my father had started writing his gospel. Now he was approaching the end. There had been days, and even a couple of weeks, when he hadn't been able to write anything. I never had that problem myself. My stories seemed to form all at once inside my head. But I guess all of us work differently.

Although he had those days when he couldn't get going, for most of the time he had stayed on a regular schedule of reading, thinking, and writing. He had read everything he could find about Jesus. He liked to think through what he was going to write even before he dipped his pen into the ink. And he had spent hours getting his stories about Jesus into exactly the right words. Yet, even though he knew that he was doing something important, I could tell that he was happy to be about finished.

He was so pleased at nearing the end of his gospel that he bought me a present one day. I've already explained that paper is very expensive here. Because of that I had been writing my stories on old scraps of paper and sometimes on pieces of broken pottery.

But in the market my father had come upon a used papyrus scroll. Someone had used it before, but apparently that person decided not to keep the paper. The roll was sold to a second-hand dealer in the market. The dealer then went through the scroll and erased everything that had been written before. The dealer did this erasing by scraping the paper with a smooth, sharp stone. That removes the ink. Of course, you can still see that something had been written on the paper. But a second-hand papyrus scroll is still a lot better than scraps of paper.

There was something else about his gift too. By giving me the scroll to write my stories on, my father was letting me know that what I was doing was important. If he had thought my stories were merely homework exercises in writing and spelling, the sort of thing children do in school, he wouldn't have spent the money for the papyrus.

It took me a couple of weeks to copy my stories on the scroll. I used my best handwriting. Even though it slowed down my work, I wanted my manuscript to look good. During that time, Father continued his writing. He was telling about Jesus' last days in Jerusalem. That was where I would have to set the last of my own stories.

Samuel's Story

(Luke 19:28-48)

"Sam, Sam," I heard my mother's voice calling. "It's time for us to go. Come home this instant. You better be ready!"

I looked into Rebecca's big brown eyes. She said that I needed to get going. I said goodbye and ran over to where my family was waiting. Luckily, since they weren't quite ready to start, my mother couldn't get too mad at me.

"Where have you been?" she asked.

I knew she didn't really care whether I gave an answer or not. She just wanted to ask the question to remind me about being on time. I picked up my pack and said, "I'm ready to go."

Rebecca is my friend. I like her a lot. We've known one another since we were babies. We have always lived next door to one another. I knew that I would miss her on this trip to Jerusalem. My family was going to the Holy City for the Passover festival. All of us Jews who can afford it want to go to Jerusalem for the holy days.

My grandfather stood up and walked to the front of our family. There were over twenty-five of us, and all were children or grandchildren of him. All of us were standing, looking at him, and ready for him to speak.

"Onward to the Holy City," he called out in his most official voice. He motioned with his arm in the direction we were to go.

Grandfather walked in front. My own father and his two brothers walked alongside him. Behind the four men came the women and children. We were going to stay with my rich uncle in Jerusalem.

Even though I am officially a boy, it will only be a couple more years until I turn thirteen and legally become a man. Because of that I can walk either with the men in front or with the women and children in the back.

At first I enjoyed the walking. I seldom leave our town. Looking at the countryside is something I almost never get to do. I liked seeing the mountains up close enough to make out the trees. The birds were calling to one another. But after nearly two hours of walking and sightseeing, we were all getting tired. I was hoping for another rest stop.

I missed Rebecca too. It's funny how most of my friends don't like girls. They tease me because I like to be with her. Of course, the girls in our town also tease Rebecca because she likes me. But she and I have always lived next door to one another. We are used to having each other around. And we have always been friends. We are probably best friends now.

Our parents know that we like one another. Since it is your parents who decide what person you'll marry, I've asked my parents to arrange for me to marry Rebecca when they pick out a wife for me. My father has said they will think about it, but he reminded me that Rebecca's parents have to decide whom they think would be best for her.

"You can't always marry the person you want to, Sam," my father said. "But don't worry. We'll either get Rebecca for you or someone else just as good."

I don't want anyone "just as good" as Rebecca. She's the girl I hope they pick for me. But there is no point arguing with Father. I'm sure he'll do the best he can.

Rebecca was sorry to see me leave. I noticed her brown eyes starting to shine with unfallen tears when I was ready to leave. But I told her not to worry.

"Really, Rebecca," I said right before we left, "what can happen in ten days?"

Our family continued on our trip to Jerusalem. On and

on we marched. After several more hours of walking, and not nearly enough stops for rest, I saw that we were near the Mount of Olives. It's right next to the Holy City. I guess it got its name because of all the olive trees that grow on it.

At this time I had walked away from my mother and was alongside my father. He and the other men were having a discussion. They were talking about the prophet Jesus.

"He's sure to come to Jerusalem for the Passover," said Uncle Jonah. "I wonder if that's the time he plans to start."

"To start what?" asked my grandfather.

"To start the revolution," Jonah answered. "That's what the Messiah is supposed to do, isn't he?"

"Rubbish," said Grandfather. "Do you really think one man is going to kick the Romans out of our land?"

"Of course not," said Jonah. "But the Messiah will lead the people of Israel. He'll be able to start the war by stirring us up. I know I'm ready to fight."

"Me too," said my father. "Just give me a sword."

Grandfather wasn't convinced.

"And what makes you think that Jesus is the Messiah?" he asked.

"He's dropped hints about it," said Jonah. "He's talked about how the kingdom of God is coming."

"I've heard him too," said Grandfather. "But he's also said that the kingdom of God is within us. Maybe he's not the sort of messiah you're expecting."

"But then what good would he be?" asked my father.

"Don't you think that God hates the Romans as much as we do?" asked Jonah, but he went on without waiting for an answer. "Of course God does. The Romans have oppressed us for almost a century now. But at last God is giving us a leader to drive them from our land. We'll be rid of them for good. No longer will this land be called by the Roman name 'Palestine.' Our land will again be 'Israel.'"

Uncle Bartholomew spoke next.

"When Jesus said that the kingdom is within us, he means that it is *within our grasp*. We only need to grab it for ourselves."

"And remember Jesus saying that the kingdom is at hand," said my father. "He's expecting the revolution any day now."

"Rubbish," said Grandfather. "You boys have missed the point of what Jesus was talking about. I've heard him too. He's not talking about setting up a different government here with our own governors, palaces, and tax-collectors taking the place of Roman ones. He's got something else in mind."

The other men were silent. I knew they didn't agree with Grandfather. But he is the leader of our family, and we have all been taught not to argue with our elders. Grandfather could also tell that his sons didn't agree with him.

"One other thing," said Grandfather. "You're too young to remember it, but you've heard me talk about it before. I've seen the Romans at war. We have had other 'messiahs' before. They get men excited and collect their own armies to battle the Roman legions. I've seen the results. I've helped bury the dead after those battles. A rebellion against Rome will lead to nothing. You boys will only get all of us in trouble."

Grandfather looked at his three sons. They remained silent but unconvinced. I didn't know whom to believe. Grandfather is the head of our family, but my father is still my father.

"What's that up ahead?" asked Grandfather pointing towards the city. "It looks like a crowd. Let's see what's going on."

We walked into the crowd. The crowd was mostly outside the gates of Jerusalem. I was still tired, but my curiosity was aroused and I felt more energetic. When we got into the crowd, we saw some men leading a donkey out of the Holy City. They brought it out to a man standing near the road into the city.

"That's Jesus," said Uncle Bartholomew. "I've seen him before."

Grandfather nodded in agreement.

Even though the men around Jesus were smiling and looked happy, Jesus himself must have been a little sad. He wasn't smiling. He looked thoughtful rather than pleased with all the commotion. But his followers were all smiles. They took off their coats and put them on the donkey to make a cushion for him to sit on. Jesus climbed onto the donkey.

The crowds cheered.

"A king, a king," they shouted. "Blessed is the king who comes in the name of the Lord."

It wasn't long before our family joined in with the rest of the people. I climbed a palm tree and pulled off some of the leaves. I tossed them to the people on the ground. They passed the palm leaves around to the other members of the family. We joined in the shouting and singing. We waved our palm leaves.

All of us joined in, except Grandfather. He stood looking at the crowds and his family. I wondered if he still thought it was rubbish.

I myself had some doubts about Jesus becoming a king, a general, or even a prince. Not that I've ever seen a king, general, or prince, you understand. But he didn't look the way I imagined one of them would. He was too calm. Too thoughtful. He waved at the crowds and didn't try to get them excited.

My father and uncles had talked about him leading armies against the Romans. But he didn't act a bit like the soldiers I've seen at home. The ones I've seen drink a lot, fight with one another, and bump into people on the streets.

It turned out that there was going to be a parade. The

crowd began to walk into Jerusalem with Jesus. We joined the parade. I moved away from our group—they were all spread out now anyway—and walked alongside Jesus on the donkey. All the time I was yelling, "Long live the king!"

Some well-dressed men whom I hadn't noticed before walked up next to Jesus.

"Master," one of them said, "get these people under control. We don't want to make a scene."

Jesus shifted his position on the donkey.

"I'll tell you something," he said. "If the people were silent, the stones themselves would cheer."

I twisted my head to glance at the stones by the road. They looked like ordinary rocks to me. How did he expect the rocks to cheer? If the stones could speak, would it be possible for them to throw themselves at the Romans? If God willed it, of course it would be possible. But was that what Jesus had in mind? I couldn't tell. Well, whatever Jesus meant, it was an odd thing for a king to say.

It was quite a parade. There had been a brief rain that morning, and so there were still a few puddles left on the road. But Jesus' donkey never stepped into any mud. People moved in front of him and put their coats over any puddle he was about to ride through. Some of us with palm branches laid them in front of the passing donkey.

Just as he was about to enter the city, Jesus stopped the parade. He raised his hand, but the people were making too much noise to hear what he was saying. However, I was close enough to hear him.

I could see that something was making him sad. There were tears in his eyes. He said something about a coming war. But instead of saying that we Jews were going to win, he talked about how Jerusalem was doomed. I knew that my uncles wouldn't like to hear that kind of talk. I hoped they were too far away to hear him.

Then Jesus looked over the crowds again. It must have

cheered him up. He waved for the people to follow him into the city. We went through the city gates. The citizens of Jerusalem came out of their houses and shops to see the parade. Hundreds joined us.

Of course not everyone was cheering. I noticed that some of the Roman soldiers looked nervous. Their fingers were clinched around the handles of swords or the shafts of spears. But they did nothing except watch.

It was about this time that I realized I was lost. Looking around in the crowd, I didn't see a face I knew. It had been a long time since my mother had waved for me to come back to her. (I pretended that I hadn't seen her.) But I wasn't too upset. The family was probably following along somewhere in the crowds. I'd be sure to catch up with one of them in a little while.

After more parading, we climbed the mountain to the Temple. It was the same beautiful building I remembered from last year and the year before. As usual, the Temple merchants were out in the courtyards. They sell all sorts of religious objects. I could tell they were doing all right. Their money boxes overflowed with silver and gold coins. My grandfather had once said that they were crooks.

Jesus must not have liked what he was seeing. After he stared at them for a minute or two, I noticed that the crowd was getting quiet. Jesus must have been angry. He jumped off the donkey, grabbed a whip from one of the merchants, and began to chase them away from the courtyards. He shouted that they were robbing the people and mocking God. He turned over their tables and poured their money on the ground.

The crowds loved it.

"Hooray for Jesus! Long live the king!"

I wondered what he would do next. But instead of marching into the Temple building itself, he went back to the donkey. I started to follow.

Before I knew what was happening, my head turned to the left. Someone was pulling my ear. I twisted my head to see who it was. As I did, I recognized a familiar arm.

"Where have you been?" my mother asked sharply. "Don't you have enough sense not to get lost?"

Opening my mouth to answer her, I was about to explain that I wasn't really lost, but I never got the chance. She noticed my little brother nearby and instantly snatched one of his ears too. She kept her fingers clamped on our ears all the way to my uncle's house. It was very embarrassing. It also made my ear sore.

That night as I rubbed my ear and tried to fall asleep, I thought a lot about Rebecca. I missed her. She and I usually spend some time with one another in the evenings. We talk about what happened during the day.

But Rebecca wasn't the only person I thought about. There was also Jesus. I had never seen anyone like him. When I remembered the tears in his eyes when he spoke of the war that he said was on its way, I felt sure that he was never going to be the Messiah to free us from the Romans. He wasn't going to lead an army. He had the makings of a prophet or a teacher but not a general.

On the other hand, I had seen him at the Temple. Jesus had acted like a king then. He had showed his anger, and his strength, when he threw out the crooks who worked there. The crowd saw that he could fight when he had to.

Jesus was too hard for me to figure out. Perhaps he would be a king. Perhaps he wouldn't. I finally decided that if he did become a king, he was going to be a different kind of king than we were expecting.

When I had decided that, I still felt sad because I missed Rebecca. Finally, when I was tired and falling asleep, I realized that I had felt sorry for myself long enough. I pretended like Rebecca could hear me whisper, "Good night. I'll see you soon."

CHAPTER 14

My father was about finished with his gospel. From start to finish he had spent almost fifteen months at work. It can take a long time to write something you'll be satisfied with.

His story of Jesus was complete except for a few more paragraphs. But he wanted to think through how he was going to end his gospel. The roll of papyrus he was writing on had only a few, white inches left at the bottom.

"Deborah, take this and read it over." He handed me the scroll with what he had written that day. "Let me know if you think that anything is missing. This tells about the last days of Jesus' life. If you can think of anything it makes you want to write a story about, go ahead."

"I'll try, but this is my least favorite part of the gospel."

"Mine too, but at least it gets better at the very end."

Susanna's Story

(Luke 19:47–23:49)

There are many different kinds of Believers: rich ones and poor ones, old ones and young ones, brave ones and ones who are afraid. And yet, even though we are all different, in another sense we are all the same. It is because of the beliefs we share that we can get along with one another. Believers are supposed to look beyond differences and love one another.

My name is Susanna. My name means "lilies." My mother says that I have a pretty name. I have one brother, Jacob.

The Believers in Jerusalem had been happy to hear that Jesus was coming to the Holy City for Passover. We were anxious to see him again. On the day he arrived, we were waiting at the city gates to greet him. But Jesus didn't come alone.

He was leading a huge parade. There must have been hundreds of people traveling with him. By the time the crowd got into the city, the numbers had grown to thousands. Everyone was cheering and shouting. We were happy to cheer with them.

But there was something strange. When we spoke to some of those shouting, they didn't really know who Jesus was. Some people were excited just because it was a parade and there were so many others in the streets. But some of the folks shouting said that they thought Jesus was going to be starting a war against Rome. They said that this was what the Messiah was supposed to do. I thought this was a strange idea because I had never heard Jesus say anything like that before. (I found out from my father later that Jesus never had said it.)

In the days right before Passover, Jesus spent much of his time teaching in the Temple. He told a number of para-

bles to those who came to hear him. He described how the world was going to end. From the way he talked, we thought he meant it was going to end right away. But, since it's still around now, he could have been mistaken about that one little thing. (Or we might have misunderstood what he said.) My mother says that although it is hard to predict the future, it is even harder to understand those who do predict it.

Often times the politicians and lawyers and teachers got into arguments with Jesus in the Temple. Not all of course. Many just sat and listened to the discussions. But there were some who wanted to fight. One of the things they did was to ask him questions which didn't have a right answer. These are the kind of questions you ask, not because you want to hear what a person has to say, but because you want to embarrass the person.

You can figure out the type of questions I have in mind. When I get mad and argue with my brother, I sometimes ask him if he's as stupid today as he was yesterday. (I make sure my parents aren't around when I do this since they don't like it.) It doesn't matter whether my brother says "Yes" or "No." No matter what he says he admits that he's stupid. That's a trick question that kids around here ask one another. I've been told that grownups ask trick questions that are even harder to answer.

I didn't always understand the trick questions that the sneaky lawyers asked Jesus. But I could tell they knew what they were doing. When one of them finished a question, he would look away from Jesus, glance at his friends, raise his eyebrows, and smile. His friends would raise their eyebrows in return and smile back.

But they weren't able to trap Jesus. He was too smart for them. He sometimes gave answers that made the people listening to the discussions nod their heads in agreement. But there were other times when he asked a question back to the people who thought that they were such smarty-pants.

I especially remember when a few of the priests, who make their living working in the Temple, asked him by what right he had thrown out the merchants. (Everyone knows that those particular merchants had been crooks, but that's not the sort of thing that we're supposed to say in public.) Jesus had done that on the day of the parade. Jesus thought for a few seconds about how to answer the question. Then he asked them a question about John the Baptist. It was something like whether John the Baptist had been a prophet sent by God. It must have been a hard question. The lawyers who were trying to trap him huddled together for a minute or so, whispering with one another. They didn't look happy when they gave their answer.

"We don't know," they said.

Jesus must have expected that response. He smiled.

"Very well, then," he said. "I won't answer your question either."

He spent a lot of time with his twelve disciples. They were almost always with him. Even though Jesus had had plenty of invitations from those of us in the city, he ate the Passover meal with his disciples. In fact, they ate the Passover at the house of a grownup friend of ours. He is also a Believer. His name is Michael.

Our friend Michael told us the story of how Jesus arranged for them to eat at his house. Michael was coming back from the well near his house. He was carrying a pitcher of water. As he neared his house, he realized he was being followed by two men. He was sure the men's faces were familiar, but he didn't recognize them.

For an instant he wondered if they were muggers. But they didn't look like robbers. Still, why were they following him? Just when he was about to enter his house, one of the men spoke.

"The Teacher said that he wants you to show us a place where he can eat the Passover."

Michael was surprised. But then he remembered that he had seen the men with Jesus. He figured he could trust them. Since Michael had heard rumors that the Romans were interested in getting their hands on Jesus, he thought that Jesus and his group probably wanted some privacy.

"Come this way," he said and showed them a room on the second floor.

That afternoon Jesus and his disciples went to Michael's house. They brought their own roast lamb and unleavened bread. They ate the dinner by themselves. Michael was downstairs. He said it was pretty quiet. But one odd thing did happen. Towards the end of the meal, someone left the group upstairs. Michael never saw who it was.

The next morning we got the bad news. Jesus had been arrested!

All of the Believers got together to discuss what we ought to do. We had tried to find out what was going on, but no one seemed to know. We heard that there had been a sword fight in a garden when the soldiers had surprised the disciples. But someone else said that Jesus had surrendered without a struggle.

The disciples had disappeared too. At first we thought they had been arrested. But that wasn't true. They were just hiding out. My mother said that it was cowardly for the disciples to hide when Jesus was under arrest. But my father said that he could never blame them for being afraid.

"I don't know what I would have done under the circumstances," he said. "God can judge them. I won't."

After hearing the various rumors, one of our leaders, I think it was my aunt, said that we'd never learn a thing by listening to all these stories. We decided to send a group over to the High Court to find out what had happened. Most of us who went were women and children. We were afraid that the Roman troops would harass any men who went.

The Roman soldiers are more likely to arrest and beat up men than women with children.

But we were too late to find out anything. The trial must have just ended. Several of the judges were smiling quietly, some looked sad and disgusted, but there were a few who were waving their arms and getting red in the face.

"We don't need to have any witnesses," shouted one of them. "We ourselves have heard him."

Next thing we knew, Jesus was led out of the court. This was the first time we had seen him that morning. He had been beaten up. His face was swollen. One eye was almost closed because of the swelling. It looked like someone had quickly washed his face before he had been taken into the court. But I could still see crusts of blood in his hair and beard.

The Roman soldiers leading Jesus away didn't seem to be paying much attention to what was going on. I don't think they cared one way or another what happened to him. But some of the priests and judges looked happy. Not all, of course, but there were some who did. You could see a few smiles and hear men saying funny things to one another. Sometimes one of them would laugh out loud. But probably most of the judges (and this is a little strange) looked like this was just a regular part of doing their job as a judge in the Roman Empire. They didn't look happy or sad.

By this time there was a large crowd following behind Jesus. In addition to us Believers, there were also people whom I didn't recognize. The crowd got bigger as we moved through the streets. Everyone wanted to see what was going on.

We followed until we arrived at Pilate's palace. Pilate is the Roman governor who is in charge of Palestine. As the crowd poured in the courtyard of the palace, I wondered why all this was happening. Why were the priests and judges doing this to Jesus?

Pilate came forward to hear the case. He asked the members of the court what they wanted.

"This man is a troublemaker," said one of the judges. "He's tearing our people apart."

"He's told us not to pay our taxes," said a thin, tight-lipped priest.

That was a lie! Only a few days before Jesus had said to pay Caesar what was due to Caesar. But the charge made Pilate raise his eyebrows.

"He claims to be our king," said a well-dressed judge.

Pilate looked at Jesus more closely. He turned to meet him face-to-face.

"Are you the king of the Jews?" Pilate asked in a tone which implied that Jesus certainly didn't look like a king. Pilate couldn't help smiling.

I didn't hear Jesus' answer. Pilate did though and shook his head. He must have thought that Jesus was partially insane.

"I don't find any fault with this man," Pilate said.

The ringleaders of the group out to get Jesus began to get worried.

"He's started riots everywhere from Galilee to Judea," said the thin priest again.

"He's from Galilee, eh?" said Pilate. "King Herod is in charge of Galilee. Take Jesus to him. This case is not in my responsibility."

The soldiers took Jesus away. The crowd followed. Herod was visiting in Jerusalem at this time and staying in a small palace near Pilate's. There wasn't room for us to follow into the courtyard. Because of that, we weren't able to hear what went on. I heard some shouting, but the words were never distinct.

After about half an hour Jesus came out. He was dressed in a royal robe and had something on his head. At first I thought that Herod had released him. But then I saw that he had been beaten up again. The thing on his head was a twisted branch from a thorn bush. Someone had shoved it on his head. The fancy clothes he was wearing were meant as a joke. Because Jesus was accused of being a king, he had been dressed up like one.

I felt sick. I was crying this whole time but didn't even know it until I tasted the salt from my tears.

Then it was back to Pilate. There were thousands of us in the crowd now. Almost everyone was against him now. Men and women laughed. From here and there came a rock or piece of garbage. People were throwing things at him.

I recognized some of the people in crowd. The very men and women who only a few days before had waved their palm branches were now shouting against him. The crowds had changed their minds about Jesus.

Pilate had a private conversation with some of the Jewish leaders. When he came out of the conference, he told us that Jesus could be set free. He didn't think that Jesus deserved to die. But many people didn't agree. A few men with loud voices began yelling, "Crucify him! Crucify him!"

Within minutes most of the crowd had joined in the chant. I could see my mother and other Believers also crying. Pilate kept trying to make the crowd calm down. It was a lost cause.

After a few more attempts to silence the mob, Pilate gave up. He called for a bowl of water. When a servant brought the bowl in, Pilate washed his hands in it.

"Listen here," he said. "Do whatever you want with this man. But remember, I'm innocent of his blood."

At that the mob cheered. Hands starting clapping. There were shouts of hooray.

Jesus was dragged away. The soldiers tossed a heavy, wooden cross on his back. He was supposed to carry it. But he wasn't able to manage it. He was too tired and in too

much pain because of the beatings. Whenever he stumbled, the soldiers hit him with the flats of their swords.

There was a black man from Africa watching this. Since there weren't many people like him in Jerusalem, he was obvious in the crowd. The soldiers grabbed him, a man named Simon from Cyrene, and made him carry the cross for Jesus.

Most of the crowd was against Jesus. Boys ran up and hit him. Men and women tossed rotten fruit at his back. You could hear people laughing.

You could also hear people crying. There was a moment, when the crowd was moving too slow for Jesus and the soldiers to get through, that Jesus stopped and turned to us.

"Don't cry for me," he said. "Cry for yourselves and for your children."

He was saying something else too, but the soldiers got things moving again and I didn't hear it.

Pretty soon we arrived at a place called Golgatha, the hill outside the city where criminals are executed. There were two robbers who were going to be crucified with him.

My father, one of the few men who went with us, asked the group of us Believers to stand together. We stood as near to the cross as we could. I prayed that God would do something to make it stop. But nothing happened. We could only watch.

Jesus didn't behave like the two robbers. They begged for mercy and screamed when their hands and feet were nailed onto the wood. They twisted around on the crosses when they were set in place. The robbers then cursed the people who were watching. But no one cared about them.

Jesus was quiet during the whole time. He didn't jerk his hands away when the nails were hammered through his skin. Only when the soldiers raised up his cross did he speak.

"Father," he said. "Forgive them. They don't know what they're doing."

Lots of people came to look at the scene. A few had something funny to say.

"If you're really God's son," said a well-dressed judge I had seen earlier, "get down off the cross. Call on some angels to help you."

Another person stood right under Jesus and turned to his friends.

"Take a look at this," he said. "Here's Jesus, the man who was able to 'save' so many others. Now he can't seem to save himself."

The man and his friends laughed.

The Roman soldiers put a sign over his head. "This man is King of the Jews," it said. The sign was meant to make fun of Jesus. But it was also meant to make fun of us, the Jewish people. Some of the priests tried to get the sign changed, but the soldiers left it up.

I never thought that human beings could be so cruel. It just wasn't right. But there was nothing we could do.

Jesus said a few things before he died. He talked with one of the robbers who was dying at his side. Their conversation lasted only a few minutes. The other thief just made fun of him.

By the middle of the afternoon Jesus was looking worse than ever. My father said it wouldn't be long now. I covered my eyes with my hands. Then Jesus said something to God. When I could force myself to look again, he was dead.

God hadn't done a thing to help him. How could God have let this happen? Didn't God care? What kind of God was this?

There were dark clouds in the sky and it looked like it might start to rain. My father had gone off when we noticed the soldiers starting to point at him. (My mother had told him to go.) Only a few of us women and children were left on Golgatha. One of the women Believers turned to those of us who were left.

"He's dead now," she said. "It's all over. We might as well go home."

So we left. The dead body of Jesus was hanging by the nails on the cross. It was starting to rain.

CHAPTER 15

Jacob's Story

(Luke 23:50–24:53)

My name is Jacob. Susanna, the girl who told the last story, is my sister. She already explained that we are Believers.

The saddest time in my life was when we left Jesus' body hanging on the cross. Our mother took hold of Susanna's hand and my hand, and then led us back home. I remember thinking that we were never going to see him again. He had always been so full of life.

But, when we had our last look at him, his dead face was pale, almost the same gray color that the late afternoon clouds have before a rain. His skin, especially around the eyes, was still puffy. The face was sad. He was as dead as dead could be. We left his lifeless body just as it started to rain. He was gone for good.

Our family went home and cried. There was nothing else to do. My sister wanted to know what had gone wrong. She wanted to know why God hadn't done something. But neither Father nor Mother had anything to say to her.

We heard from other Believers that the twelve disciples had disappeared. Had they now been arrested or were they still just hiding? Nobody knew.

One of the richer Believers decided that Jesus' body shouldn't be left out on the cross overnight. Joseph of Arimathea—that was his name—went to Pilate and asked permission to take the body and bury it. Pilate gave his approval. Joseph and his servants took the body down and buried it in the tomb Joseph had planned to use for himself.

Joseph was an old man. He often said that he didn't have that much longer to live anyhow. He told people that since he knew this he had made all the plans for his funeral. He didn't want his family to make a fuss when he died. Joseph had picked out a fine cave near the city to be his tomb. He had chosen it because it hadn't been used before and because it was next to a large garden. He said that he liked the view.

The evening after Jesus' death we Believers got together. We needed to make plans for the future. We went quietly to our meeting place. My father said that we needed to do things without attracting attention. It was possible that the Romans might arrest us. He went holding Susanna's hand. I followed about ten minutes later with my mother.

When we Believers met, I noticed that there weren't as many of us in the house as there usually were. Less than half the men had come. Father said they had good reason to be afraid of the Romans. But I wondered if that was the whole story.

"Jesus is dead and gone," said our neighbor Ruth. (She sounded as if she were about to cry.) "What will we do without him?"

"I had hoped for a new world," said Uncle James, my mother's brother. "It was going to be a world of peace and justice. But what is left for us now? I can't even keep my dreams."

"I know how you feel," said Rahab, an old woman who was the only great-grandmother in our group. "When he was alive, I felt like the world was a good place. But after what we saw, I'm tired of life. Maybe it's time to put this religious stuff behind us and get on with what's left of life."

Some of the Believers agreed with Rahab. They said we

might as well give up the whole idea of believing that Jesus was the Messiah. The Messiah wasn't supposed to die.

"Maybe so," said my father. "But we still must serve our God. Besides that, Jesus is not totally gone. We can still keep him in our hearts. His memory can continue with us."

"Memory may be good enough for you," said Rahab. "But I can't remember things as good as I used to. If Jesus isn't around, it doesn't make any sense to look to him for anything."

"But we should try!" said Susanna. (She's not afraid to speak up.) "Jesus wouldn't have told us about things we could never hope for."

"I used to think so too, child," said Uncle James sadly. "But Jesus wasn't able to take care of himself. He couldn't stop the Romans from killing him. You were there, child. You know what happened. You saw it. I only heard about it."

The adults talked back and forth about this for several hours. Susanna was the only one of the children who spoke, but she was the oldest one there. We wondered where the disciples were. They had been closer to Jesus than any of the rest of us. Yet no one had heard from them.

Finally, when it was very late, the adults had some very long prayers. (Most of the kids had fallen asleep.) There were silent prayers and prayers said out loud. We asked God to be with us.

When the prayers were done, the Believers agreed on a plan. We decided that we would try to live as Jesus had said to. No one said that it was going to be easy. The fellowship we enjoyed together was something we didn't want to give up.

We also said that Jesus had shown himself to be one of the great prophets like Isaiah or Jeremiah. It was too bad that he had been killed as they had been. His death had proved that he was not the Messiah. But he was still a great man.

Some of the people who have become Believers after all this happened can't understand why we acted the way we did. They ask us why we didn't believe that Jesus was going to die and then rise from the dead. That's what he said he would do. My father and mother have come up with the best answer I have heard.

"Unless you had been there," they say, "you can't imagine what the crucifixion was like. You have to try to understand what it was like for us. We saw him suffer. We watched the tears come from his eyes and the blood trickle down his skin. He looked so very helpless. None of us who had known him and loved him could even think that he was going to return to life."

And that isn't all they say in answer.

"The prophecies about the resurrection that are so clear to you now were not at all clear to us then. We hadn't known what Jesus had been talking about. Even those people who thought that Jesus was talking about himself and his own death weren't sure about how we were supposed to take his words."

The next day, a Sabbath, was miserable. The Believers did not get together as a group. Everyone wanted to stay at home. We got more bad news too. Our neighbor Ruth told us that one of the disciples was dead. She didn't know which one. The rumor was that this one had killed himself.

There were other stories about the disciples. But no one knew where they were. Pilate had sent some soldiers to guard the tomb where Jesus was buried. I guess he thought that someone might steal the body.

Some of the women planned to go the next day, Sunday, and properly prepare Jesus' body for the tomb. On the day he had been killed, there had been a hurry to get Jesus buried before the Sabbath began. Joseph of Arimathea and his servants hadn't finished cleaning the body or completed wrapping it in the burial cloth. Susanna said it wasn't decent to leave him like that. When my mother heard about this plan to bury Jesus properly, she decided to go along with the other women.

Early on Sunday morning, just before the sun came up, my mother left with the other women. Even though other societies, like the Egyptians, have professionals who prepare bodies for burial, women have that job in our culture. The women looked sad as they waited outside our house for my mother. They had been crying a lot.

About an hour after they had departed, right before my father was leaving for work, my mother flung open the front door and shouted, "He's alive! He's alive!"

"Who's alive?" I asked.

"Jesus! Jesus!" she exclaimed. "The angels told us that he had come back to life."

My father, who up until this time had only looked sad, now looked worried. I could tell that he was nervous.

"Calm down, Darling," he said. (His voice sounded as if he were afraid.) "Why don't you lie down and have a little rest?"

He went over and gently took hold of her arm.

"There, there," he said, patting her arm.

My mother shook his hand away. He was trying to figure out what to do next. Mother was very excited. She was speaking much faster than usual.

"When we got there," she said in a voice which almost bubbled with excitement, "we noticed that the large stone that blocked the entrance to the tomb had been rolled away. We saw that the soldiers who were supposed to be on guard were sleeping on the ground. We couldn't make sense of it.

"We were going into the tomb, but we couldn't see the body anywhere. Suddenly there was a flash of light. Two men in white stood beside the tomb. I can tell you that we were afraid. One of the men asked us what we were doing there. 'Why do you seek the living among the dead?' he asked. 'Don't you know that Jesus is alive?'

"I'll tell you right now that we were too frightened to speak. 'Do you remember,' the man, I mean the angel, asked, 'that he told you he would be killed by sinful men and then rise up on the third day?' Now as soon as he asked us that last question, I remembered that Jesus had said something like it in Galilee.

"Next thing we knew, the men were gone. We knew we had to tell people about what had happened. Joanna and Mary had heard a rumor about where the disciples were hiding. That's where they went. The other Mary went to her family. I came straight to you. Isn't it the greatest thing you've ever heard?"

My mother was so excited that she didn't notice the strange look my father was giving her. He looked a little sick.

"Why don't you sit down, Darling?" he asked.

She looked at him like he was speaking a foreign language.

"What's gotten into you?" she asked. "I have to tell the others."

She went to the door before we could stop her or even speak to her.

"I'll be back soon," she said and slammed the door.

Then she was gone.

"I wonder if they searched the tomb," said my father to himself quietly. He then turned to the two of us. "Jacob! Susanna! You both need to listen to me. Your mother has suffered a lot during these last three days. Try to comfort her. Make her get some rest. Don't let her get too excited. I'll stop back here later in the day."

He left for work. He didn't want to leave, but your job is your job. He was sure my mother had been seeing things. By that I mean to say that she was seeing things that weren't there. He couldn't believe that Jesus had come back to life.

But by late afternoon he had changed his mind. One of the disciples—I think it was Peter—came out of hiding and said that he had seen Jesus that very day. The other women who had been to the tomb told the same story as my mother.

That night the Believers came together for another meeting. Ten of the disciples were there too. I recognized most of the group, but there were a few visitors to Jerusalem we didn't know. That didn't matter to us though. Believers are to accept one another as sisters and brothers, even when they're strangers.

Everyone was excited. The men and women who had seen Jesus told their stories. After some reading of the Scriptures, we sang some songs. We couldn't sing very loud though. We were still afraid that the Romans might be looking for the disciples.

Suddenly Jesus was in the room. I didn't see him walk in the door. And I hadn't heard a boom of thunder or seen a flash of lightning. One minute he wasn't in the room. The next minute he was. Despite the fact that I had been hearing stories about Jesus coming back to life, when I saw him standing there, I was afraid. I thought he was a ghost. Other people must have been thinking the same thing.

"Don't be afraid," he said. "I'm no ghost. Come and touch me. See for yourselves that I'm really alive."

I was still scared. But looking at his strong, happy face made me lose most of my fear.

"Do you have anything I could eat?" he asked one of the disciples.

Someone handed him a piece of fish. Jesus ate it. Right then I knew that he was really alive. If I know one thing about ghosts, I know that they don't eat fish. Jesus wasn't a ghost. He was a man. He was a man who had died and was now alive.

Jesus then began talking to us. He cheered us up. He talked and laughed and sang like he had always done before.

Jesus disappeared and reappeared many times during the next forty days. He spoke with the disciples. He talked with some of the learned Believers. Of course he also talked with us younger ones as well.

Finally the day came when Jesus said he was going to leave us. He led the disciples, the Believers, and many other people into the hills outside Jerusalem.

While he stood on a hillside, he told us what he expected us to do until he came back again. We were to keep our hopes up. We were to trust that God would be with us. At the end of his talk he told us to go and tell other people about what he had showed us.

When he finished his message, we realized that this was a goodbye meant for a long time. Some people cried.

"Don't worry about the future," he said. "I'll always be with you."

He was at the top of the hill when he said goodbye. The clouds were heavy that day. One of the clouds came in lower than the others and covered him at the top of the mountain. When the cloud moved away, he was gone.

At first I wasn't able to understand what he meant when he said that he would be with us. That just wasn't possible. He wasn't with us. On the other hand, Susanna says that he is with us when we gather together and remember him. Sometimes when I pray or show kindness to another person, I feel like he's right beside me. It's funny.

Of course I can't touch him or see him like I used to. But I know that he's around. I can tell you that he really is alive.

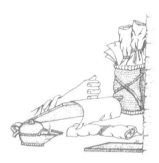

"Well, Deborah," said my father. "Are you satisfied with your work?"

I said I guessed I was. He had finished his gospel on the same day that I had finished mine. It had taken longer than I had thought it was going to take, months longer in fact.

Spread open on the table where we had been writing were the papyrus sheets that held our two gospels. With the tip of a clean finger I tested to see whether the ink on mine was dry. It was. I rolled my papyrus up. I slid my scroll across to him.

"Well, Father, we're done." We smiled at one another. He wrapped the two scrolls neatly into rolls. I tied the ribbons to keep them tight. "Now we'll have to see if anyone ever wants to read what we've written."

191